# The Volunteer Development Toolbox

Tools and techniques
to enhance volunteer
and staff effectiveness.

Marilyn MacKenzie and Gail Moore

**Partners Plus** is a management consulting firm specializing in training and consulting services to the voluntary and public sectors. The partnership offers the combined strengths of respected and experienced leaders in the field. Their mission is to act as a catalyst in the growth and enhancement of volunteerism in Canada. The firm works with staff and leadership volunteers in national, provincial and local organizations. Partners Plus is the major distributor of voluntary sector publications in Canada and publishes a newsletter, *Partners in Print,* with subscribers from coast to coast.

### Books by Partners Plus:

MacKenzie
*Dealing With Difficult Volunteers* (1988)
*Curing Terminal Niceness* (1990)

MacKenzie and Moore
*Building Credibility With The Powers That Be* (1990)
*The Volunteer Development Toolbox* (1993)
*The Group Member's Handbook* (1993)

### Our Services:

• Consultation • Training • Keynote Presentations •
• Program Development •
• Distribution of Leading Publications •
• Development of Manuals and Training Programs •

**9030 Leslie Street, Suite 220, Richmond Hill, Ontario L4B 1G2, Canada
Telephone (905) 886-8585 • Fax (905) 886-9151**

ISBN # 0-911029-41-9

© Marilyn MacKenzie and Gail Moore, 1993

Published by:

Heritage Arts Publishing
1807 Prairie Avenue
Downers Grove, Il. 60515 U.S.A.
Office: (708) 964-1194
Fax: (708) 964-0841

# Purpose

The Volunteer Development Tool Box was created to help you, leadership volunteers and staff, teach others about the principles and practices of volunteer management. The reality today is that many people who work with volunteers have had no formal training in the effective mobilization of this important resource. **Enter the Toolbox!** It contains tools created not only by Partners Plus but by leaders in our field. The Toolbox will assist you in developing a strong and effective volunteer force. It is designed to promote active learning - a chance to try out the tool and to talk about its unique application in your own agency. The format also includes background theory that will build the confidence and competence of the session leader.

Nothing in this Toolbox is written in stone! The suggested forms and procedures are guidelines only, so feel free to adapt and adopt those that enhance volunteer satisfaction and performance. The forms may be duplicated for use within your agency without obtaining copyright permission.

Most importantly, we hope you will enjoy working with the material in the Toolbox and that you will return to it frequently as your program develops and new issues arise. We think the elements, carefully introduced and nurtured, will create a thriving and successful volunteer program. Best of luck!

Gail Moore and Marilyn MacKenzie
Partners Plus, 1993

This book is lovingly dedicated
to our husbands,
Murray MacKenzie and Hugh Moore
for their unfailing support.

# Table of Contents

# Chapter One

## INTRODUCTION

### Why Volunteer Management?

At last, the importance of volunteer effort in the life and health of communities is being accorded the attention it has long deserved. The need for a systematic approach to the management and mobilization of volunteers becomes urgent, not only because more people are becoming involved but because the problems they strive to address are increasingly complex, the needs continue to mount and the time available to volunteer is compressed.

Just as an orchestra performs more harmoniously under the direction of an attentive conductor, and a football team wins more games with effective coaches, volunteer performance is enhanced when thoughtful direction is offered. Effectively harnessing volunteers' talents and skills, while being responsive to their individual needs, clearly requires coordination.

Without volunteers, many worthwhile programs, initiatives and projects would not take place. Because volunteers are so vital to organizational success, we must ensure effective recruitment and retention practices. Volunteers may be coordinated and managed at the local level by:

- paid staff coordination or unpaid volunteer coordination
- a volunteer board member assigned to the task
- the vice-chair of each committee coordinating the group
- volunteer teams specifically responsible for recruitment or recognition
- a volunteer development committee spearheading the effort.

To win volunteer commitment and to ensure volunteer satisfaction, everyone has a role to play in sound volunteer development.

- from the Executive Director who acknowledges the value of volunteers by hiring and promoting staff who work well with volunteers;

- to the Board who establishes a volunteer philosophy statement and standards of volunteer practice in their agency;

- to the front line staff and volunteers who work alongside new recruits to form a service team;

- to the receptionist who answers volunteer and client enquiries.

## Title:  The Volunteer Retention Cycle

*Purpose:*

This model allows us to see both "the big picture" of supporting volunteers as well as the individual steps required in the volunteer development process.

Often people mistakenly believe that: "All we need are people.  If we had more people, we'd have no problems".  Much attention is lavished on recruitment.  Working with volunteers is like looking after a car.  To keep the car in top running condition, you must take it in regularly for service, keep it filled with gasoline, make repairs and replacements as needed, adapt to changing conditions and treat it with affection.  Your responsibility does not end with selecting the automobile.  So too with volunteers!  Working with volunteers is more than recruiting.  It includes all those activities that enhance volunteer satisfaction and improve volunteer performance.

*When To Use This Model:*

This model is the foundation for all activity in effectively working with volunteers.  It provides a framework for making decisions about what needs to be done at different stages of the process.

- When introducing staff or volunteers to effective volunteer management as a process in your organization.

- In volunteer and staff orientation.

- When introducing a new component or concept on volunteer management to demonstrate its fit in the overall process.

- As a summary, to bring people together on a shared vision of how volunteer management might be structured.

- In written form, to begin a volunteer development manual.

*How Long:*

Allow twenty to thirty minutes to present and discuss the model.

*How to Use It:*

- Display the retention model on an overhead or flipchart.  Distribute a copy to each individual, inviting them to make notes on their own copy.

- Outline the key elements of the model, stressing the internal core - "the heart of volunteer management - assessing, coaching and recognition."

- Lead a full group discussion on the importance of the model for your agency.

## *Key Concepts:*

1. The model responds to the current trends for a more professional and comprehensive approach to volunteer management.

2. Effective volunteer management is a process that involves discrete phases or steps plus a fundamental base that is ongoing - assessment, coaching and recognition.

3. Eliminating any phase of the retention cycle will reduce the effectiveness and satisfaction of the volunteer.

## *Sample Questions:*

1. How does this model contribute to volunteer satisfaction and effectiveness?

2. What would happen if we eliminated any one of the steps in the Volunteer Retention Cycle?

3. Why is there so much attention to recruitment in the voluntary sector? What would this model suggest?

4. What, in your opinion, are the factors influencing volunteer retention?

5. How do we use this model in working with volunteers in our agency?

## The Volunteer Retention Cycle:

## A Look at The Model

Look first at the overall design of the model. It is two circles, one within the other. Just outside the bigger circle are the pre-recruitment activities, steps that help you get ready to go to the community for volunteer support. The circle revolves through the phases of recruitment, asking people to take on a project, making sure they understand the task and feel comfortable with it. Every volunteer will need a basic orientation to your agency, what it does, how it operates and how their tasks fit into the overall mission or plan.

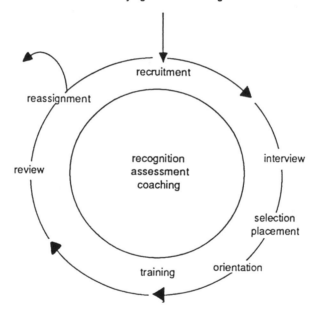

Volunteer Retention Cycle
Pre-Recruitment: Building Program Support
Assessing Readiness
Determining Program Goals
Identifying Volunteer Assignments

An extended phase of skill development may include several chances to learn more about the task assigned and how performance can improve. As a project winds to a close, there is a final review that may lead to a reassignment to the same task or a new assignment. The volunteer may choose to take a well-deserved "sabbatical" or join another organization to develop new and different skills. We need to encourage them to move on if this is the right step for them. After all, you want to be sure that people feel as good about their departure from your agency as they did during their involvement. In that way they can talk with their friends about the merits of helping out and can choose, perhaps at a later date, to return.

What makes this model unique is the inner circle. Recognition, coaching and assessment are the very heart of effectively working with volunteers. The Volunteer Retention Cycle suggests that the core features are continuous, ongoing from the start of the cycle until its end. They undergird all other phases. In other words, recognition is not a "terminal event", something done only when the volunteer chooses to leave or you try to dislodge her. It happens throughout the volunteer experience. Coaching is not a single speech, delivered pep rally style ("We know you can do it! Rah! Rah!") at the start of a worthwhile project, but is an element of each get together, shaping progress towards mutually held goals. Assessment is not a final reporting to you of how you did, but rather a regular check up - how are you doing? How are you feeling? What help do you want?

Volunteers need thoughtful tending if they are to really thrive in their tasks. You want them to stay with the organization and perhaps to take on new tasks because they have enjoyed their past experiences so much. This doesn't just happen.

# An In-Depth Look at the Volunteer Retention Cycle

## Pre-Recruitment: A Planning Step

### Building Program Support

Before bringing new volunteers into your agency or before starting a new program that involves volunteers, consider the adjustments that may be needed when new people join.

- Is our organization ready to welcome new people with new/different ideas?
- Does the staff feel that introducing volunteers is a good idea?
- Is there support for this program amongst the Board, our staff, our clients?
- Are volunteer policies in place to ensure fair treatment?
- Are we clear about the need for the program in our community?

### Assessing Readiness

Sometimes current volunteers feel torn between keeping life within the organization as it always has been - comfortable and familiar - and welcoming others with different perspectives, ideas and purposes. New people may suggest change, disruption, a sense of discomfort. This reluctance, whether by staff or volunteers, may be very confusing for new recruits. The argument goes something like this:

| Yes, we want new volunteers | BUT ... | We don't want to change. |
| We need more help here | BUT ... | We only want volunteers who are available 9 to 5. |
| We welcome new ideas | BUT ... | We tried that idea seven years ago and it didn't work. |

Volunteers receive mixed messages. Some people, sensing the confusion, decide not to stay because they prefer clear cut situations where they feel they can make a contribution. Others may feel that the double messages are directed at them "We want volunteers, but we don't want you." They leave, feeling very unhappy about their experience.

Few new people agree to stay on and work with a group that is experiencing confusion. New people haven't built the relationships or the history that compel them to stay. Current volunteers, who have both history and relationship, feel that the failure of the new volunteer to stay proves that the new recruit lacked commitment. They view all future recruits with a suitably jaundiced eye.

### Determining Program Philosophy Goals and Needs

* Do we agree on the program purpose and goals?
* Have we planned the introduction of the program to increase the likelihood of its success?

### Identifying Volunteer Assignments

* Do we know what kinds of jobs need to be done to make this program successful?
* Do we know how many people are required to carry out the required tasks?
* How must existing position descriptions be modified to meet current, local needs?
* Can we identify the skills, knowledge and interests required for these tasks?
* Where might we find volunteers who would enjoy doing the tasks we offer?

### Recruitment

There is a magic formula that increases the likelihood that volunteers will be effective, will enjoy their work and will stay with you. It is "selecting the right volunteer for the right job at the right time so everybody wins". Recruitment in the 90's means seeking out those individuals with the necessary skills, knowledge and attitudes to do the jobs needed by the organization.

## Interview

Some people resist the idea of interviewing prospective volunteers, believing it takes too much time or seems too formal. This phase of the retention cycle, however, is critical in truly understanding the volunteer's goals and dreams for this assignment. Taking time initially to get to know the volunteer often avoids misunderstandings in the future. Volunteers who are listened to, not just talked at, feel valued and understood.

## Selection and Placement

After an interview, most volunteers are comfortably placed in a program, committee or position of their choice. Occasionally a clear fit does not exist.

- A volunteer wants to take on a task that seems unrealistic at this time (a young man without experience insists he wants to be the President of your Board).

- The volunteer may have goals that cannot be met at the present time (a symphony volunteer wants to bring classical music into local daycares. While this is a desirable goal, it is not a priority budget item at this time).

- The volunteer's responses to the interview make the interviewer reluctant to place a volunteer (a gentleman who claims Vitamin B controls diabetes would like to join that organization's local board to promote Vitamin B to the community).

In these situations, you cannot place the volunteers in the position of their choice.

- In the first circumstance, you may suggest a minor role as you assess his skills, working with a more senior person to expand his understanding and develop his competence at your agency. He may become a President in the future.

- In the second situation, you may re-direct this volunteer to another project. Be up front that you can't achieve this dream with your current budget.

- You don't want to encourage a volunteer to take action against policy. Adherence to policy is an essential element of being a volunteer. You would injure the reputation of the agency if this person was allowed to speak on behalf of the organization. A polite thank-you but no thank you would be appropriate. No placement is wise at this time.

Selecting volunteers to act in the best interests of the clients is a big responsibility.

Many agencies have elaborate screening procedures, including police checks, that protect clients from harm. It is common practice to check references, especially when you feel uncertain or ill at ease.

## Orientation

The purpose of orientation is to help the new volunteer feel comfortable, competent and safe as quickly as possible. The focus of orientation should be on the information the volunteer needs to know to do her job today. More elaborate historical data, future plans, detailed documents can be introduced once the volunteer understands the "lay of the land".

## Training

The purpose of training is enhanced job performance and increased personal satisfaction. Training can be delivered in a variety of formats, not just in a formal workshop setting.

## Coaching, Assessment and Recognition

These three core elements are fundamental to all the interactions between volunteers and those who work with them, both staff and volunteer leaders.

## Coaching

Coaching can be done in a relationship of equals, and this is most appropriate for working with volunteers. A coach helps you set standards, assists in the development of strategies and identifies the need to adjust and adapt plans. The responsibility for performance, however, rests with the volunteer. The coach focuses on performance and results, allowing the volunteer the freedom to act.

## Assessment

Volunteers are still uncomfortable with the term "evaluation". Assessment suggests an ongoing process of checking. It allows the volunteer to determine what changes need to be put in place to achieve the desired results. Tiny "course corrections" along the way are more fruitful than a terminal evaluation that tries to uncover why something didn't work.

## Recognition

As a core concept, recognition attempts to find volunteers doing something right. Rather than focusing on the awards, banquets and grateful speeches delivered once a year, it focuses on the informal aspects of recognition - the heartfelt thank you, the pat on the back, the handwritten note, the phone call that says "you were missed".

Each phase of the volunteer retention cycle works in harmony with the others to see that volunteers enjoy their volunteer experience and have opportunities for personal growth. At the same time, attention to the cycle reduces or eliminates problems before they start. Putting systems in place that support volunteers strengthens all aspects of your volunteer program.

# Chapter Two

## Title: What are the Trends and Issues Shaping Volunteerism?

### *Purpose:*

To identify the trends and issues facing voluntary organizations today and explore how we can creatively respond to those trends so as to more effectively recruit and retain volunteers.

### *When to Use This Exercise:*

Schedule this exercise at the beginning of a volunteer or staff development meeting. Prior to actually recruiting for jobs, this exercise will help staff or volunteers understand how to design work that is more responsive to people's changing expectations.

### *How Long?*

Allow 45 minutes to an hour for this exercise.

### *How to Use It:*

- Read the accompanying theory handouts "Trends and Issues Shaping Volunteerism" and "Creatively Responding to Changing Trends".

- Page 11 provides a summary of the key concepts. Enlarge each section to make overhead transparencies.

- Begin with a brief presentation on current trends, highlighting the key points with the overhead transparencies.

- Break people into small groups of 3-5. Give them the handout on "Trends and Issues" as well as the "Trends Worksheet". Ask each group to discuss these trends and what they as staff or volunteer leaders are doing in response to them. Allow 15 - 20 minutes for this discussion. When assigning the discussion, ask each group to start with a different trend, so that all will be covered.

- Facilitate a full group discussion of how our organization can respond to these trends. Distribute the handout "Creatively Responding to Changing Trends" and lead a discussion of any additional responses that did not emerge from the groups themselves.

- Conclude the session by having people talk in pairs about what they learned and how they will apply these concepts in their recruitment or management efforts.

## Key Concepts:

- Greater demand for volunteer services results in increasing competition for volunteers.

- Erosion of the traditional base of volunteerism requires that we broaden our recruitment efforts. Working women, youth, baby boomers, sandwich generation, seniors - all have unique talents to offer and needs that challenge.

- People have limited time to volunteer.

- People expect interesting assignments and to be treated professionally.

- Volunteers are less tolerant of authoritarian management and bureaucracy.

- Patterns of work are changing - large numbers of skilled, unemployed, people working at home with greater flexibility, people taking early or forced retirement.

- Increasing cultural diversity means that we must develop strategies to reach out and extend the invitation to volunteer. Our organizations must better reflect the diversity of our communities.

## Sample Questions:

- What are we currently doing in our organization that reflects these changing trends?

- What additional responses might we consider implementing to be more attractive to potential volunteers?

- What are the implications of ignoring these trends in the design of volunteer opportunities?

- What opportunities are available for people who want to volunteer outside traditional daytime hours? Who provides orientation and supervision?

- Does our organization reflect the demographics of our community? What might we do to change this?

### Greater Demand for Volunteer Services

☐ increasing number of registered charities
☐ greater competition among organizations
☐ aging population requires more services
☐ people have more options and choices

### Erosion of Traditional Volunteer Base

☐ decrease in traditional daytime volunteer
☐ volunteers represent diverse backgrounds
☐ youth population declining
☐ baby boomers, sandwich syndrome
☐ seniors are recruitment opportunity

### People Have Limited Time

☐ short term, project oriented
☐ job sharing to create manageable chunks
☐ group activities provide social outlet
☐ quality of time, not quantity

### People's Expectations about Volunteer Work are Changing

☐ more demanding about nature of the work
☐ want meaningful, interesting assignments
☐ expect to be treated professionally
☐ interested in issues and causes
☐ dislike large, bureaucratic structures
☐ avoid authoritarian management

### Increasing Cultural Diversity

☐ be responsive to changing demographics
☐ develop strategies to reach out
☐ people want to access power
☐ opportunity to contribute to community
☐ involvement in decision making process

### Patterns of Work are Changing

☐ growing numbers of skilled unemployed
☐ increasing number working from home
☐ people taking early retirement
☐ increasing number of women in workforce

| Trends Worksheet | |
|---|---|
| **Trend** | **Responses** |
| Greater demand for volunteer services results in increasing competition among organizations. | |
| Erosion of traditional base of volunteerism - working women, youth, sandwich syndrome, seniors. | |
| People have limited time to volunteer. | |
| People expect interesting assignments and to be treated professionally. Less tolerant of authoritarian management and bureaucracy. | |
| Patterns of work are changing - skilled unemployed, work at home, early retirement. | |
| Increasing cultural diversity means we must develop strategies to reach out, extend invitation. | |

# Trends and Issues Shaping Volunteerism

☐ Demand for volunteer services is growing dramatically, with a critical need to expand the volunteer base. With government cutbacks and fiscal restraint, organizations are attempting to meet greater needs with fewer resources. This increased demand results in greater competition for volunteers, and so people have more options than ever available.

☐ Increasing demands on time, with changing work and leisure patterns are resulting in people having very limited time to volunteer. One-parent families, both parents working, aging parents - all leave people with little discretionary time. Many of today's volunteers are looking for shorter-term assignments and the resulting sense of achievement that comes from completing a task. A recent U.S. study (National Volunteer Center and J.C. Penney) found that 79% of those not volunteering would be more likely to volunteer if the task was short term.

☐ There is growing dissatisfaction with large bureaucratic structures. Change in large organizations seems slow and unresponsive. People prefer to join smaller organizations, locally controlled, where their effort can make a visible difference. Large organizations need to explore how that feeling of freedom to act can be maintained, and how a sense of achievement can be demonstrated.

☐ Volunteers today expect challenging, interesting assignments that involve work they enjoy doing. The older Baby Boomers (40's) are looking for meaning, values, and enrichment in their lives. Their search for meaning finds expression in their volunteer work.

☐ Today's volunteers come from a much broader cross-section of our society, with a growing number of professionals, young people, the unemployed. Organizations today are increasingly targeting their recruitment efforts to better reflect the diversity of our communities. This means recruiting beyond our own circle of friends and identifying outreach strategies that involve people from other cultural and socioeconomic groups as well as those with very different points of view.

☐ Unemployed people are entering the volunteer ranks in unprecedented numbers, often bringing excellent skills. Some are between jobs and are looking for opportunities to keep their work experiences fresh and updated. They need to volunteer for resume building. Their involvement may be of short duration, until the right job appears. Some are early retirees who were perhaps unprepared to abandon the workforce. They use volunteering as a substitute work experience. They may look to come in at nine a.m. and leave at five p.m., expecting staff to be available to counsel and direct them when they feel they need it. Both groups may come with bruised self esteem that volunteering can help to heal.

☐ Today's volunteers expect to be treated professionally. They bring the expectations of the business sector to their volunteer life. Some organizations must alter their approach to the way the volunteer base is managed. It is critical to have a clearly defined job for volunteers to do, to provide training and support for volunteers, especially volunteer leaders and to evaluate performance and progress. Management systems must be put in place that recognize and support volunteer involvement.

☐ New views of leadership and management have particular significance for voluntary sector groups. People are less tolerant of an authoritarian management style. Instead they seek leadership that mobilizes people, and gives them freedom to be creative in finding solutions. Many leaders are struggling with the balance between enabling others to act and taking responsibility to see that work is done.

☐ The increase in the numbers of seniors will continue to dominate both the demand for and the delivery of volunteer services. Currently, fewer seniors are choosing to volunteer than other age groups. Senior volunteers bring unique needs and wishes to the volunteer experience. They are retiring younger, are healthier and have more leisure time options open to them than ever before. It is important to adapt current programs to be responsive to the seniors in our population, since this group of skilled, capable people offers a marvellous recruitment potential.

## Creatively Responding to Changing Trends

**Episodic Volunteers**:  Assignments that allow for service of short duration, usually 3-4 months or less.  **One-time**, the volunteer who gives service only once, and **Recurring**, the volunteer who works on a project that recurs each year.  The short-term work might be done by individuals or even a group of people (service clubs, teen groups, etc.).  More information about episodic volunteers is found in Chapter Five.

**Job Sharing or Team Volunteering**:  Volunteer work is divided among two or more people.  Traditional approaches to work are questioned and creative solutions to flexible time arrangements are made.  This approach is particularly effective for leadership positions that have significant time demands.

**Group Volunteering**:  An entire group is the volunteer unit - family, church group, business department, youth, clubs, etc.  The group subdivides the work.  Start by recruiting one lead member who in turn "persuades" the rest.

**Ripple Effect Recruitment**:  Based on the theory that those people already connected to your organization (current volunteers, their friends and relatives, clients, friends and relatives of clients, staff, donors, people in the neighbourhood, retirees in the field), are the best targets for a recruitment campaign.

**Recruitment Team**:  Group of people who are enthusiastic about your mission, who have excellent recruiting and communication skills, and who with appropriate training work as a team to plan for and carry out volunteer recruitment.  This could be a subgroup of the people or committee responsible for volunteer development.

**Targeted Recruitment**:  Specific groups are approached who would benefit from volunteering with your organization and a recruitment message is shaped to appeal to these people specifically.  The best recruiters are people from that specific group.  A corporate retiree would be the best route to other retirees, a teen would be preferable to an older person recruiting teens.  Chapter Five provides additional information.

Two target groups in particular offer significant opportunities for effective recruitment.  Volunteers from the corporate world bring access not only to skills but to other resources.  Organizations who want to tap into this segment of the volunteer market will need to have a professional approach and offer attractive work that meets people's varying needs for recognition, personal growth, status, and a balance from work pressures.  When the assignments can also build a sense of group fun and commitment, it is a win-win situation.

Retired people are drastically underutilized as volunteers.  Organizations who focus their recruitment efforts in this area must be aware of the differing needs of older adults, providing not only challenging opportunities for them to use their considerable skills and experiences, but also recognizing that with retirement people expect to have flexibility to travel as well.

**Flexible Service Hours and Locations**: Rethink when and where volunteering might be done. Some projects can easily be done by people working at home. Much can be accomplished in the evening or on a weekend if space is available for the volunteer. Remember, the majority of current volunteers work full or part-time.

**Removing Barriers to Volunteering**: In today's competitive market, organizations are recognizing that volunteering must be accessible to people. This means that policies must be in place that provide for reimbursement of expenses. People on fixed incomes, the unemployed and younger volunteers will be attracted to organizations who reimburse them for out-of-pocket expenses.

**Job Simplification**: Traditionally onerous jobs can be divided or streamlined so that it is easier to recruit people to handle different parts of the responsibility. Organizations today are re-evaluating the long term commitments required to serve in certain roles, especially leadership ones.

**Blending Social Functions with Effective Meetings**: Meetings are kept short and productive. As an option before or after the meeting, people are invited to an informal coffee and networking session. Those who feel pressed for time need not attend.

**Training in Effective Volunteer Management is Part of all Leadership Training**: It is understood that working effectively with volunteers is an important role of volunteer leaders. Opportunities for learning about working with volunteers are built into staff and volunteer leadership training.

# Chapter Three

## Title:  Why Do People Volunteer?

***Purpose:***

To identify a range of reasons why people volunteer and to explore the importance of understanding these reasons for effective job design and placement.

***When To Use This Exercise:***

This exercise is a good warm up to a discussion of recruiting and managing volunteers today and may be used in a variety of ways.

- Staff or volunteers responsible for recruiting and managing other volunteers will enhance their understanding of volunteer motivation and thereby their effectiveness in mobilizing volunteer resources.

- Volunteers in your organization may appreciate an opportunity to discuss their own and other's reasons for volunteering, thus gaining a deeper understanding of themselves and their colleagues.

***How Long:***

Allow 15 minutes to complete all phases of this activity.

***How to Use It:***

- Distribute the work sheet "Why Do People Volunteer" to each person or display it on a flipchart or overhead.

- Working alone, ask people to choose in order of preference the three main reasons they volunteer or in the case of staff, why they believe people volunteer.

- Suggest that they then share their choices with a neighbour or small group.

- Lead a full group discussion of the importance of their observations and ideas.

***Key Concepts:***

- People volunteer for very different reasons.

- The same person may look for different things at different times in his or her life.

- In designing a volunteer job, ask what the person is looking for - don't assume you know.

- The most frequently stated reasons why people volunteer are:

  a) being involved in an issue of importance or a cause in which they believe

  b) a sense that they are needed and valued

  c) meaningful work that interests them

- Successful volunteer assignments include these elements.

***Sample Discussion Questions:***

1. What were your own three top reasons for volunteering?

2. Were your reasons different from those in your group? Why might this be so?

3. Are your reasons for staying involved as a volunteer different from why you initially joined?

4. What does this tell us about assigning volunteer jobs in this organization?

5. What kinds of questions might help us discover what a person is looking for in offering to volunteer? Answers you might expect would include:

   a) Tell me about a volunteer experience that was important to you.

   b) What do you picture yourself doing when you think about volunteering?

   c) What are the strengths or interests you feel you bring to volunteering?

   d) Why did you choose to come to our agency?

# Why Do People Volunteer?

_____     Good working conditions

_____     A sense of being needed and valued

_____     An opportunity for personal growth

_____     Meaningful work that interests or challenges
people

_____     A sense of obligation

_____     A chance to use special (unique) skills

_____     Fellowship, socialization, friendship

_____     Recognition for work well done

_____     A caring and compassionate supervisor

_____     A chance to be involved in decision-making

_____     A feeling of being involved in an issue of importance, a cause in
which people believe

_____     Career or work experience

_____     School or course requirements

_____     Giving something back in gratitude

_____     Belief about the importance of helping others

_____     Meeting expectations of people whom you hold in
esteem

_____     Relief from personal negative feelings

## Instructions:

To make transparencies, enlarge each section by 150 - 200%.

## Motivational Type: Achiever

*Goal: Success in a situation which requires excellent or improved performance*

**Positive Attributes**

- ☐ concern with results, personal best
- ☐ sets goals, takes risks
- ☐ innovative, restless
- ☐ likes to be challenged
- ☐ likes to work alone

## Motivational Type: Power People

*Goal: To have an impact or influence on others*

Influencing Change For Social Good

**Positive Attributes**

- ☐ tries to shape opinion
- ☐ wants to change things
- ☐ exercises power to benefit others
- ☐ concern for position, respect, reputation
- ☐ may be charismatic
- ☐ verbally aggressive, forceful

## Motivational Type: Affiliator

*Goal: To be with others, to enjoy mutual friendships*

**Positive Attributes**

- ☐ seeks out relationships
- ☐ likes to work with other people
- ☐ sensitive to feelings, needs of others
- ☐ supports others in achieving goals
- ☐ talks about feelings

# Title:  Motivational Analysis

### *Purpose:*

To determine the preferred style of a volunteer, acknowledging that people with different styles prefer different kinds of supervision, recognition and job placement.

### *When To Use This Exercise:*

This exercise is particularly useful for volunteer leaders in discussing the retention of volunteers today or in preparing to chair committees.  It is also most appropriate for people preparing to interview and place volunteers.

### *How Long:*

Allow an hour to complete all phases of this activity.

### *How To Use It:*

*   Read the accompanying theory handout "Understanding Volunteer Motivation" as well as the motivational charts in this chapter.

*   Briefly introduce McClelland's theory that three different forces act as motivators, acknowledging that although most of us are a mix of all three types, one tends to dominate. You may want to identify the three types by name.

*   Ask people individually to complete the Motivational Analysis.  When finished, they score their answers turning the page and marking whether each answer was Power, Achievement or Affiliation.  They should then tally the numbers for each motivating force.

*   Lead a full group discussion on the results.  Share with the group more information about the three types outlined in the theory.  You may want to illustrate these descriptions with overhead transparencies produced from page 20.

*   If time permits, break into groups of like types, and discuss the following questions:

    1.   What kind of supervision or direction do you prefer when you are assigned work to do?

    2.   What kind of recognition is most welcome?

    3.   What jobs in our organization do you find most satisfying?

    4.   What advice do you have to help others effectively with your particular motivational type?

Give groups about twenty minutes to discuss before reporting back to the larger group.

- Hand out the Motivational Type Worksheets (pages 25-27).

- Conclude with a full group discussion of the importance of understanding motivational types for volunteers working together (see Theory Material).

### Key Concepts:

- No one style is better than another.

- Effective teams benefit from a mix of styles.

- Individuals are a mix of styles but one tends to dominate.

- People's motivational styles may change over time.

- Different styles prefer different kinds of placement, supervision and recognition.

- Determining one's preferred style can lead to an enhanced volunteer experience.

- An understanding of styles allows volunteers to adapt their own styles to make all team members feel confident and comfortable.

### Sample Discussion Questions:

1. What was your dominant motivational type?

2. How does your type affect your preference for supervision, recognition and volunteer job choice?

3. What happens when your supervisor or volunteer boss is of a different motivational type?

4. Why is motivational type an important concept for volunteer leaders/staff to know?

5. What suggestions do you have for using this information about motivational types in working with volunteer committees?

# Motivational Analysis

Each of the following questions has three choices. Choose the one in each question which most closely fits your own motivations. Remember, there are no wrong answers. Place an "X" before the letter of your choice.

1. _____ a. When doing a job, I seek feedback.
   _____ b. I prefer to work alone and am eager to be my own boss.
   _____ c. I seem to be uncomfortable when forced to work alone.

2. _____ a. I go out of my way to make friends with new people.
   _____ b. I enjoy a good argument.
   _____ c. After starting a task, I am not comfortable until it is completed.

3. _____ a. Status symbols are important to me.
   _____ b. I am always getting involved in group projects.
   _____ c. I work better when there is a deadline.

4. _____ a. I work best when there is some challenge involved.
   _____ b. I would rather give orders than take them.
   _____ c. I am sensitive to others - especially when they are mad.

5. _____ a. I am eager to be my own boss.
   _____ b. I accept responsibility eagerly.
   _____ c. I try to get personally involved with my superiors.

6. _____ a. I am uncomfortable when forced to work alone.
   _____ b. I prefer being my own boss, even when others feel a joint effort is required.
   _____ c. When given responsibility, I set measurable standards of high performance.

7. _____ a. I am very concerned about my reputation or position.
   _____ b. I have a desire to out-perform others.
   _____ c. I am concerned with being liked and accepted.

8. _____ a. I enjoy and seek warm, friendly relationships.
   _____ b. I attempt complete involvement in a project.
   _____ c. I want my ideas to predominate.

9. _____ a. I desire unique accomplishments.
   _____ b. It concerns me when I am being separated from others.
   _____ c. I have a need and desire to influence others.

10. _____ a. I think about consoling and helping others.
    _____ b. I am verbally fluent.
    _____ c. I am restless and innovative.

11. _____ a. I set goals and think about how to attain them.
    _____ b. I think about ways to change people.
    _____ c. I think a lot about my feelings and the feelings of others.

Source Unknown

**Motivational Analysis** (cont'd)

1.  a. Achievement
    b. Power
    c. Affiliation

2.  a. Affiliation
    b. Power
    c. Achievement

3.  a. Power
    b. Affiliation
    c. Achievement

4.  a. Achievement
    b. Power
    c. Affiliation

5.  a. Power
    b. Achievement
    c. Affiliation

6.  a. Affiliation
    b. Power
    c. Achievement

7.  a. Power
    b. Achievement
    c. Affiliation

8.  a. Affiliation
    b. Achievement
    c. Power

9.  a. Achievement
    b. Affiliation
    c. Power

10. a. Affiliation
    b. Power
    c. Achievement

11. a. Achievement
    b. Power
    c. Affiliation

## Motivational Types Worksheets

| Motivational Type | Description | Conditions of Supervision |
|---|---|---|
| **Achievement-Oriented**<br><br>Goal: Success in a situation which requires excellent or improved performance. | Positive Attributes:<br><br>• Concern with excellence/personal best<br><br>• Sets moderate goals, takes risks<br><br>• Enjoys a level of moderate stress<br><br>• Restless/innovative<br><br>• Likes challenging work<br><br>• Likes to work alone<br><br>• Likes to overcome barriers<br><br>Negative Attributes:<br><br>• Will sacrifice people to achieve goals<br>• May be insensitive<br>• Can be autocratic<br>• Gets bored quickly | • Wants concrete feedback to improve performance<br><br>• Likes results-focused management<br><br>• Wants a boss who leaves him/her alone<br><br>• Likes to be challenged<br><br>• Enjoys time management and responds to goals, objectives and conceptual thinking<br><br>• Needs a well-delegated task<br><br>• Enjoys being consulted about decisions, planning |

| Motivational Type | Description | Conditions of Supervision |
|---|---|---|
| **Affiliation-Oriented**<br><br>Goal: To be with others, to enjoy mutual friendships. | Positive Attributes:<br><br>• Seeks out relationships<br><br>• Likes to work with many people<br><br>• Likes social activity for its own sake<br><br>• Sensitive to feelings, needs and wants of others<br><br>• Supports others in the achievement of their goals<br><br>• Talks about feelings<br><br>Negative Attributes:<br><br>• Will sacrifice project goals to keep people happy<br><br>• Concerned about personal popularity<br><br>• Hates to discipline<br><br>• Is crushed by criticism | • Wants a concerned, caring supervisor<br><br>• Enjoys long chats<br><br>• Welcomes advice<br><br>• Likes to be part of a team, pair, group<br><br>• Needs help if situation is tense or unpleasant<br><br>• Avoids conflict<br><br>• May not report problems back to supervisor or may "dump" them back to supervisor |

| Motivational Type | Description | Conditions of Supervision |
|---|---|---|
| **Power-Oriented**<br><br>Goal: To have an impact or influence on others; to bring about change. | Positive Attributes<br><br>• Concern for reputation, position, respect<br><br>• Tries to shape opinion<br><br>• Wants to change things (eg. opportunities for the physically challenged)<br><br>• Combative, fighting spirit<br><br>• Verbally forceful<br><br>• Uses Social Power:<br>- Exercises power to benefit others<br>- I win - you win<br>- Charismatic<br>- Creates confidence in group that are able to achieve goals<br><br>Negative Attributes<br><br>• Uses Personal Power<br>- I'm in charge<br>- I win - you lose<br>- Group is dependent, submissive<br>- Treats people indifferently<br>- Autocratic | • Likes clear cut policies and procedures<br><br>• Likes to know limits of authority<br><br>• Likes strong leadership<br><br>• Needs lots of personal freedom and respect<br><br>• Works well alone<br><br>• Tends to operate outside standard rules and regulations<br><br>• Likes to associate with other "power brokers"<br><br>• Needs to be included in decision making and planning |

# Understanding Volunteer Motivation

Researchers David McClelland and John Atkinson suggest that there are three different forces that act as motivators to human behaviour. Although they acknowledged that most individuals have a mix of all three types, one tends to dominate. The three types identified are:

| | |
|---|---|
| **The Achiever:** | This person is committed to accomplishing goals, welcomes a challenge and looks for opportunities to test out new skills and improve performance. |
| **The Affiliator:** | This person values relationships, enjoys working with others and seeks out opportunities to be helpful and supportive. |
| **The Power Person:** | This person seeks to influence people and events so that change is realized. |

No one style is better than any other. In fact, most successful projects require a mix of styles to blend the work of a group. Teams made up of a variety of styles benefit from the different perspectives people bring to the task. However, people with different styles prefer different kinds of supervision, recognition and job placement. It is helpful to determine the preferred style of a volunteer in order to provide an effective match.

In attempting to explain the differences among the three styles you might think of the example of the person who joins a Toastmaster Club.

The Affiliator would suggest that she joined because she enjoyed the people in the group and looks forward to the luncheon meetings. She might volunteer to be on the social committee.

The Achiever joined so she will be more confident in her various leadership roles and would like to win the award for best new member performance.

The Power Person plans to run for political office and would like to persuade the Toastmaster Club members to support her campaign. She is especially interested in the environment issues.

The charts on pages 25-27 outline the motivational types, their positive attributes and some of the possible negative consequences of each type. Remember that people are rarely one type to the exclusion of all other characteristics. This chart is a simple guide. People are much more complex than this guide would suggest.

It is important to note that in our culture, there is real discomfort with the notion of "power". Its presence is often noted as a criticism rather than a compliment. McClelland in a later work, "The Two Faces of Power", described power in two ways:

**Personal Power**: This is our more negative description of power. The individual wants to be in charge, the boss. She is more motivated by personal ambition than the welfare of others. This person prefers associates who will be submissive and responsive to her vision of reality.

The individual who is motivated by a need for personal power views power as a finite commodity. By sharing power, information or control with you, that person fears she has less power for herself.

**Social Power**: This is a more positive view of power. The individual exercises power for the benefit of all. She wants to make changes to help others. There is a genuine concern for the welfare of all players on the team. Some of our greatest world leaders and politicians would be found in this category - Sister Theresa, Martin Luther King, Gandhi, John Kennedy, Jean Vanier. These people believe power is infinite. In sharing power, information or control with you, they believe we are all stronger.

As you review the chart more carefully you will discover some of the challenges faced by staff and leadership volunteers as they try to coach and direct volunteers of a different motivational type:

The volunteer who is an affiliator is looking for a patient, chatty supervisor who really cares about how the volunteer is feeling about the assignment. The supervisor who is an achiever is just anxious to get on with it.

The affiliator is concerned about any conflict, while the achiever is so focused on the goal to perhaps be unaware of conflict within the group.

The affiliator may perceive criticism as a personal attack rather than a simple suggestion directed at enhancing performance. The achiever believes that everyone is anxious to improve performance and would welcome such a suggestion.

Both the affiliator and the achiever may find the power person too honest, forthright and "pushy".

The power person loves political intrigue, the affiliator hates it.

The affiliator chairs a meeting that attends to the needs of the group. The decisions are secondary. The achiever is happy only if the agenda is covered, decisions are made and the meeting ends on time. Power people only come to the meetings that they think are worthwhile. Yours may not be one of them.

Adapted from a description by Marlene Wilson in
*The Effective Management of Volunteer Programs.*
Volunteer Management Associates, Boulder, 1976.

# The Importance of Motivational Types for Volunteers

Obviously, staff and leadership volunteers need to understand their own styles and the potential negative attributes that may be misinterpreted by volunteers with whom they work. They also need to appreciate the styles of others and make allowances or modifications in their own behaviour to make all team members feel comfortable and confident. Some suggestions for harmonizing styles:

✓   Talk openly about differences in style.

✓   Ask people about their preferred supervisory style and be sure to demonstrate an effort to deliver that kind of supervision.

✓   When new groups form, have people talk about motivational styles and their own expectations. Establish mutually agreed upon ground rules that address style issues.

✓   Ask someone who is a distinctly different style to coach you in meetings or on projects. An affiliator vice-chair who agrees to monitor the process of a meeting can be a real asset to an achiever or power person.

✓   Look for compromise opportunities to meet a variety of motivational needs. A work meeting of ninety minutes that has a clear, tight agenda will appeal to those who are task-oriented. This can be followed by an optional leisurely social time that will appeal to those people with strong needs for affiliation.

✓   Place people in positions that complement their motivational needs. Someone who longs for social interaction would prefer working with a group, not alone in a back office. If someone hates meetings but is interested in your cause, don't ask him to attend endless meetings. Use people's best skills and interests.

✓   Make your own needs known. There are creative solutions to your discomfort. If your concerns are pleasantly presented, most people are prepared to work with you when recognition is made of the value of different motivational types.

✓   Welcome different approaches to problems and solutions. Comment on the value of different perspectives. Leave a clear message that different is desirable.

✓   Be patient, someone else may be confused or frustrated by your style.

# Chapter Four

## Developing Systems and Supports

## Title: Building a Resource File

### *Purpose:*

- To identify current contacts and their connection to your organization
- To help select suppliers and resources as needed for your group
- To identify those groups who might be willing to volunteer for short term projects
- To identify gaps in your current contact list

### *When To Use This Exercise:*

At least once annually review this exercise. Be sure to include newly active members in the discussion. Before any project, check through the file for leads. If you are initiating a totally new venture or trying to "crack" a new territory, start with this exercise.

### *How Long:*

The list generation takes about 25 minutes. Recording and updating is the time consuming part. You might approach a computer student to help you.

### *How To Use It:*

- Invite a cross section of people from your group to participate in a brainstorming session. Try to get a representative sample that reflects the diversity of your organization. Eight people is an ideal size for such a group.

- Ask people to list all the organizations with which they are personally connected. Stimulate ideas by listing categories on the flipchart. Include schools, churches, business connections, voluntary groups, service agencies, service clubs and professional associations.

- Then ask people to complete a similar list of contacts for their own immediate family. Do not exclude any group because you have not worked directly with them before.

- In groups of four, share your lists, eliminating duplicates. Identify a contact within your organization for each group and an external contact affiliated with that group, along with a current phone number. More than one contact is always welcome.

- Post your results for all to see! You will be amazed how many potential networks you can now access.

- Transfer results to 3 x 5 cards for your resource file or better yet create a computer listing by category for easy access. Keeping your resource file up to date is important if it is to remain a useful tool. Annually circulate the list to the inside contact person. Are they still willing to be the contact? Is the information listed still relevant?

### Variation:

If you are recruiting a specialized group, invite people with particular knowledge in the area required. Ask them to identify others you might approach to become involved. Ask permission to use their names in recruiting these people.

When you have completed this exercise you may discover important gaps in your current resource list. You can now set out to identify a connection by asking someone who is likely to have that connection.

### Key Concepts:

- It is easier to recruit people you know or who have a personal connection with your organization.

- Your group has many contacts and connections that are not being approached.

- Updating the contact list is important.

- People in the community will help if asked.

- You can access groups if you can identify a contact.

### Sample Discussion Questions:

1. How many different contacts did your group identify?

2. What surprises did you discover?

3. How can we use this information in our agency?

4. How can we best keep it up to date?

Adapted from *Marketing Magic for Volunteer Programs*
by Sue Vineyard

# Title: Developing a Recordkeeping System

**Purpose:**

To develop a volunteer records filing system that is inexpensive and simple to maintain.

**When To Use:**

The trend today is to computerized information systems that support volunteer recordkeeping and statistics. The collection of anecdotal information, however, usually does not lend itself to this system. This is a simple way to record and save pertinent information at any time.

**How Long:**

Once the system is organized, it only takes a few minutes to use it on any occasion.

**How To Use It:**

- The system consists of a set of 9" X 12" envelopes with the opening flap on the longer horizontal side. They are filed alphabetically in a hanging file or records box.

- Consider recruiting an office volunteer to organize the system.

- Use an envelope for each volunteer, labelled at the top corner with name and telephone number. The envelopes are then arranged alphabetically in a place that you can easily access.

- When the volunteer starts with your organization, keep any forms, personal information, copy of the Window of Work, etc. in the file.

- Whenever you observe a volunteer accomplishing an exceptional task, doing something commendable or dealing effectively with a particularly difficult situation, not only comment verbally but make a brief note about it and drop it in the volunteer's file. For example:

    - A new volunteer makes an excellent suggestion about orientation that you are excited about implementing. You might ask the volunteer to record the key suggestions and then slip a dated copy of the memo in the volunteer's file.

    - You observe a volunteer handling an unpleasant situation tactfully and sensitively. In addition to verbally expressing your admiration, file a brief descriptive note with the date.

- A committee chair planned and organized an exceptional Annual General Meeting. Simply jot the person's name on a copy of the agenda (or meeting announcement) and file for future reference.

- A volunteer helped design a new recruitment brochure. Be sure that a copy goes in his file.

## Key Concepts:

• An effective recordkeeping system is a basic element of effective volunteer management.

• A system that is simple to maintain will be used regularly.

• Volunteers can be encouraged to provide positive feedback for other volunteers.

• Anecdotal recordkeeping provides a foundation for effective volunteer recognition.

• Anecdotal records provide excellent information for reference letters, placement reports, support documentation for personal applications, letters of commendation and personal thank you notes.

• When volunteers resign their files can be stored away, but readily available for future reference.

# Title: Creating a Volunteer Opportunity Book

*Purpose:*

To help in recruiting, interviewing, orienting and placing volunteers, develop a scrapbook with pictures of volunteers involved in their work on one side and typical position descriptions on the other.

*When To Use This:*

The Volunteer Opportunity Book can be used as part of an initial recruitment conversation; in a placement interview or when re-assigning volunteers after a project ends. You might want to leave it in your office reception area so that visitors will have a sense of the activities of your group and may be stimulated to volunteer.

*How Long:*

Five or ten minutes of browsing through the book will be helpful.

*How To Use It:*

- Identify someone in your group who likes to take pictures. Be sure to provide film for the camera and cover any expenses.

- The photographer takes pictures of people volunteering. Include behind the scenes photos and a broad range of volunteer activities as well as special events. It is wise to take photos that reflect different ages, sexes and cultural backgrounds so that you display a welcoming attitude to everyone. Include two or three pictures for each job category. Most importantly, show people having fun.

- Create one page descriptions for the tasks done by these volunteers, highlighting some of their activities. See the sample job description for suggestions of what to include. Remember the "no surprises" school of volunteer development. Be honest. Please remember that the descriptions are only guidelines of possible activities and need to be negotiated with each volunteer. Identify how this work benefits the mission of the organization.

- Use a photograph album to display the pictures on one side and the highlights of these various responsibilities on the other. When people come to be interviewed or if you go to them, have the book available when you are describing the work of your group and possible volunteer placements. The book may also suggest highlights of your organization's year. Give people time to look at the book on their own and be ready to answer questions.

## Key Concepts:

- People are often unaware of the range of choices available for volunteering.

- Many people respond better to pictures than print material.

- An opportunity to browse through the book before the interview acquaints the prospective volunteer with an overview of your services. This reduces the time you have to spend describing your organization.

- In combination with The Window of Work, you can identify skills and interests needed for specific jobs that will appeal to volunteers.

- This book is an excellent orientation tool for new volunteers.

- The development of a Volunteer Opportunity Book might be an excellent initial task for a Volunteer Development Committee.

## Sample Discussion Questions:

1. What are the benefits of a Volunteer Opportunity Book in your organization?

2. How might you use it?

# Chapter Five

## Creative Recruitment

## Title: Creating Challenging Volunteer Assignments

### *Purpose:*

- To assist in recruiting people with the appropriate skills, attitudes and knowledge.
- To clarify for current volunteers, the responsibilities of each person's job description.
- To examine volunteer jobs that require a huge time commitment and streamline them to make them more manageable,
- To reduce gaps and overlaps in the work to be done.

### *When To Use This Exercise:*

- In training people how to develop volunteer assignments.

- The person responsible for recruiting and/or managing volunteer resources will want to work on the creation of volunteer assignments before recruitment begins.

### *How Long:*

In a training setting, allow a half to one full hour for each description. You may find that people initially have difficulty with the purpose and job responsibilities. They tend to focus more on how they do the job rather than the what.

### *How To Use It:*

- Meet with 2 or 3 people who are doing the job or who have just completed the task. Distribute the Volunteer Assignment Outline.

- Review what is meant by each one of the categories listed (you may want to refer to the sample Volunteer Assignment Outline - viewed on an overhead, written on flipchart paper or used as a handout).

- Ask people to develop their own position description - emphasize the purpose, job responsibilities that describe what people do, not how they do it and skills, attitudes and knowledge required. Keep the description to no more than 2 pages.

- Collect results. You will need to editorialize results for consistency, but be sure to get permission from the group.

### Key Concepts:

- People need a clear outline of what is expected of them if they are to succeed.

- Specific attention to required skills, attitude and knowledge will help you determine how and where to target your recruitment efforts.

- Most people enjoy the freedom of how they will organize their own work once they understand what goals are desired.

- Understanding the purpose of an activity shapes all other behaviours.

- A volunteer assignment in an honest outline of what is expected and what constitutes success.

- Each volunteer assignment is negotiated with the volunteer at the time of recruitment and placement.

### Sample Discussion Questions:

1. Does this position description clearly outline what is expected?

2. Does the work as described overlap with existing positions? How so?

3. How will this person know when she/he has been successful?

4. What training must be put in place to make this person successful? Who is responsible to see that it is completed?

5. Does the person who is designated to supervise this position understand his/her role?

| Volunteer Assignment Outline | |
|---|---|
| **Title:** | |
| **Purpose:** | |
| **Job Responsibilities:** | |
| **Skills, Attitudes, Knowledge:** | |
| **Relationships/ Liaison:** | |
| **Time Commitment:**<br>   # Hours:<br>   Term:<br>   Peak Time: | |
| **Benefits and Challenges:** | |
| **Success Measures:** | |
| **Training:** | |

## Volunteer Assignment

| | |
|---|---|
| **Title:** | *Youth Volunteer Basketball Coordinator* |
| **Purpose:** | *To plan and implement a weekly basketball league for boys and girls ages 10-16.* |
| **Job Responsibilities:** | *1. Draws up schedule for basketball teams.*<br>*2. Ensures that all necessary equipment is available.*<br>*3. Assigns referees and senior volunteer observers.*<br>*4. Reports accidents, injury damage and disturbances.*<br>*5. Identifies outstanding players for MVP awards.* |
| **Skills, Attitudes, Knowledge:** | • *love of basketball*<br>• *good organizational skills*<br>• *commitment, follow-through, responsible to attend weekly*<br>• *enjoys working with youth*<br>• *communication and problem-solving skills* |
| **Relationships/ Liaison:** | • *Reports to Senior Program Staff-Youth on duty* |
| **Time Commitment:**<br>  # Hours:<br>  Term:<br>  Peak Time: | *Games: Thursdays 4:30 - 6:30 (must be present)*<br>*2-3 hours per month planning/communicating*<br>*1 hour per week reporting/recording* |
| **Benefits and Challenges:** | • *First time we've had this position*<br>• *Free membership to Youth Program Leaders Club*<br>• *Letter of reference available upon request*<br>• *Builds leadership/problem solving skills* |
| **Success Measures:** | • *All matches are posted 2 weeks before game*<br>• *All equipment safely maintained and available at start of each game*<br>• *All critical incident reports are filed on the day of incident* |
| **Training:** | • *MVP awards are given to 2 participants each session*<br>• *Level 1 Coaching*<br>• *Leadership training* |

## Title: Target Analysis

### *Purpose:*

To assist in creating a focused recruitment strategy for volunteer jobs. Clearly identifying the specific skills, attitudes and knowledge required helps pinpoint the most appropriate places to look for volunteers.

### *When To Use This Exercise:*

This exercise works well prior to recruitment efforts or at a nominating committee meeting.

### *How Long:*

Analyzing the targets for each volunteer position takes about 20 minutes. A Nominating Group or Recruitment Team can become quite proficient at using this technique and can compress the time required.

### *How To Use It:*

- Meet with two or three people who are doing the job or who have just completed the task. Distribute the Volunteer Assignment Outline for the position.

- Confirm the skills, attitudes and knowledge sought. It sometimes helps to create a character who would be ideal for the position.

- List places where you will find people with the necessary skills. For example, if you want to recruit a Treasurer for your group, you might approach an accounting firm. In a rural setting, list the specific people in your community with these skills or like skills.

- Using your Resource File, what contacts already exist to connect with these people? See sample Target Analysis. Rank these options in priority order.

- Determine what you can offer that might encourage the person to volunteer - is it a chance to meet new people, is it business contacts for someone just starting out, is it real life experience for a student?

- If you discover you have no current contacts, you will need to strategize about how to establish a contact that will have a real payoff for you. What networks will lead you to the people you need?

- Decide who will contact the person identified.

### Key Concepts:

- Recruitment efforts that are focused to a specific target group will be more successful than a broad appeal.

- Identifying the benefits for the potential volunteer prepares you to recruit.

- Pre-existing contacts can help you seal a commitment to volunteer.

- Recruitment doors are usually easier to open when you have a contact on the inside.

### Sample Discussion Questions:

1. What are the benefits of using Target Analysis prior to recruiting?

2. If you had no contacts in the area of the job description, what networks might you approach? How would you do this?

3. How might we use this activity in our group?

# Target Analysis

1.  **Who am I looking for?  What skills, attitudes, knowledge do I seek?  (Go for the IDEAL)**

    _____

    _____

    _____

2.  **Where might I find large numbers of people who have the necessary skills?**

    _____

    _____

    _____

3.  **What contact(s) do I already have to these people?**

    _____

    _____

    _____

4.  **What might I offer to this person that would be valuable to him/her?**

    _____

    _____

    _____

# Target Analysis

## *Vice President, Publicity and Promotion*

---

1. **Who am I looking for?  What skills, attitudes, knowledge do I seek?  (Go for the IDEAL)**

   *Personable, good communication skills, understanding of our work, public relations skills.*

---

2. **Where might I find large numbers of people who have the necessary skills?**

   *College public relations course, public relations department of industry, government, hospitals, small P.R. firm, community health organizations.*

---

3. **What contact(s) do I already have to these people?**

   *Jim - has a brother who is a college instructor*

   *Marlene - her husband has just started a P.R. firm*

   *Bob - Executive Director of major industry in town*

---

4. **What might I offer to this person that would be valuable to him/her?**

   *College - real life experience*

   *P.R. firm - contacts, visibility, recognition on all print material*

   *Industry - recognition on all print material, acknowledgement as corporate sponsor*

---

## Title: Episodic Volunteer Worksheet

*Purpose:*

To identify a range of short term tasks that are appropriate for people who want to volunteer on a one shot or occasional basis.

*When to Use This Exercise:*

To develop short term opportunities that will be attractive to people with limited time, invite a selected group of current volunteers and staff to meet and discuss the issues. This would be especially appropriate before launching a recruitment drive.

*How Long?*

This exercise will require approximately one hour.

*How To Use It:*

- Read the theory in this section as well as Chapter Two. Prepare flipchart sheets with headings titled "One Shot Assignments" and "Recurring Assignments".

- Ask participants to identify ways in which volunteers are currently involved on an occasional basis, recording their ideas on the flipchart sheets.

- Present a brief theory overview emphasizing how the development of episodic volunteer opportunities is a creative response to today's trends.

- Break into two groups, asking one to identify the potential benefits of involving more volunteers on a short term basis and the other to identify the potential pitfalls in expanding the range of short term opportunities. Allow ten minutes for this.

- Facilitate a full group discussion, soliciting additional input from participants. Record the key findings for future consideration and discussion.

- Distribute the Episodic Volunteer Worksheet to half the group and ask them to discuss additional ways in which volunteers might be involved on a short term basis. Distribute a volunteer assignment for which it is difficult to recruit to the other half. Because these jobs are often cumbersome and complex, ask them to consider how to restructure the job to make it appropriate for episodic volunteers. Allow 15 - 20 minutes for this activity.

- As each group reports back the ideas generated, record on flipchart paper.

- Should time permit, the group could discuss the seasonal nature of episodic assignments, using the chart on page 48.

- If the group is enthusiastic about the potential of involving more volunteers on an episodic basis, invite interested people to form an ad hoc group to review the information from the session and propose a plan of action.

### *Key Concepts:*

- Volunteer work that is short term will be attractive to people with limited time.

- People often say they are not volunteers because they don't have time.

- Episodic volunteer jobs may attract people who have never considered volunteering before.

- Redefining the work to be done is the first step in developing episodic opportunities.

- People who enjoy a short term volunteer assignment may be more likely to say yes to another opportunity at a later time.

- Episodic opportunities are especially appropriate for groups.

### *Sample Questions for Discussion:*

- What are the benefits to our organization of involving volunteers in short term projects?  What are the potential pitfalls?

- How might our traditional volunteers feel about an influx of people who only volunteer for a short while?

- What concerns might staff have about expanding episodic opportunities?

- How would screening, orientation, training, supervision and recognition be different for episodic volunteers?

- What systems do we need to put in place if we develop an episodic program?  What resources would this require?

- How can we involve staff and current volunteers in developing episodic volunteer opportunities?

## Episodic Volunteer Worksheet

*Trend:* People have limited time

*Creative Response:* Short-term volunteer work

| Description | One-shot assignments of short duration | Short-term assignments that recur regularly/annually |
|---|---|---|
| Current short-term volunteer jobs | •<br><br>•<br><br>•<br><br>•<br><br>•<br><br>• | •<br><br>•<br><br>•<br><br>•<br><br>•<br><br>• |
| Additional short-term jobs that we could develop | •<br><br>•<br><br>•<br><br>•<br><br>•<br><br>• | •<br><br>•<br><br>•<br><br>•<br><br>•<br><br>• |
| Tasks that might be done by a group of people | •<br><br>•<br><br>•<br><br>•<br><br>•<br><br>• | •<br><br>•<br><br>•<br><br>•<br><br>•<br><br>• |

## Seasonal Episodic Opportunities

| Time of Year | Individual Volunteer Opportunities | | Group Activities | |
|---|---|---|---|---|
| | One Shot/Short Duration | Recurring | One Shot/Short Duration | Recurring |
| Fall | | | | |
| Winter | | | | |
| Spring | | | | |
| Summer | | | | |

# Episodic Volunteers

Limited time to volunteer is the reality of today's world. A study revealed that more people would volunteer if tasks were shorter. The challenge for us is to more creatively redefine the work to be done so that we can take advantage of these largely untapped resources.

**Volunteer work that is of short duration.**

These activities involve one-time service only and might include helping at a one-day event or agreeing to work on a project that will take a few months.

**Volunteer work that occurs at regular intervals.**

These activities involve service that is short-term in nature and which recurs at regular intervals. Here volunteers experience the satisfaction of completing an assignment or project and then have an option of doing it again at another time. This approach has the added benefit of cutting down on repeated orientation times.

Volunteers who serve on an episodic basis may have formal volunteer assignments. At the same time, many opportunities to volunteer informally are not viewed as part of the formal volunteer management system.

**Episodic volunteers can be used when:**

- The person is available for only a few days or weeks:

  - a student between school and a summer job
  - a recently retired executive planning to travel extensively

- A specific skill set is needed to perform a highly specialized task:

  - a quilter teaching students during an arts festival
  - a computer specialist to install an accounting system

- A group of volunteers are needed to carry out a task that requires limited skills but lots of "warm bodies":

  - collating a newsletter
  - preparing kits for conference participants

Adapted from *Episodic Volunteering*
by Nancy Macduff

# Implementing an Episodic Volunteer Program

**Recruit an advisory committee** of volunteers,staff, members and/or clients to plan and implement the program.  They will provide valuable advice and insights as well as becoming your biggest supporters and proponents for the program.

**Conduct a needs assessment** of staff, current volunteers, previous occasional volunteers and clients.  Before doing the assessment, research the following:

- Current volunteer involvements
- Priority recruitment needs
- Any past history of using occasional volunteers
- Anticipated benefits of an expanded episodic program

**Develop a plan** to implement the program:

- Be clear about the goal or purpose of the program
- Identify specific objectives, describing the steps to be taken
- Plan for the intake, orientation and recognition process
- Consider how you will evaluate the program

**Build suitable assignment descriptions** that:

- Identify new tasks suitable for short-term involvement
- Redesign current volunteer jobs by:
  - breaking them into smaller segments
  - delegating parts of them on a short term basis
- Identify the skills that people will need to be successful

**Market the episodic opportunities** through the target analysis strategy outlined in Chapter Five.  Identify the skills required and consider where you will find these people.

Focus on the short term nature of the involvement.  This may appeal to retirees who want to be free to travel, young mothers home with children, career professionals, students, and other volunteer groups like churches, service clubs and membership associations that often enjoy one-shot opportunities to do something together as a group.

Adapted from *Episodic Volunteering*
by Nancy Macduff

# Title: Recruiting Practice

## *Purpose:*

To help leadership volunteers, group members and/or staff who work with volunteers become more effective recruiters by engaging in recruiting conversations.

## *When To Use This Exercise:*

This exercise will help prepare recruiters to be successful.

## *How Long:*

The full activity takes about 1 hour. The exercise should be done after volunteer assignments and target analyses are completed. Many organizations are using recruitment teams to recruit for leadership positions as well as program volunteers.

## *How To Use It:*

*   Read the accompanying background material on Recruitment.

*   Have people talk to one another about how they were recruited. You might start in pairs giving each person 2 to 3 minutes to tell his/her story. Re-create new pairs to talk about their most effective recruitment experiences.

*   Invite individuals to share their stories. Try to end with a very successful experience.

*   Ask the group to reflect on what makes for effective recruitment. You will want to list their answers on a flipchart.

*   Have the group break into pairs again but this time ask each person to recruit the other to his/her volunteer position. Each person will need about 10 minutes for this portion of the exercise.

*   Ask how many were successful. Be prepared to discuss what helped people recruit successfully and what made the activity more difficult.

You might expect:

| Helpful | Not Helpful |
|---------|-------------|
| - knowing the job | - pressure of time |
| - my own positive experience | - distractions |
| - the person's understanding of the organization | - job didn't match volunteer interest and skill |
| - listening and answering questions | - already overcommitted |
| - a friendly smile | - lack of enthusiasm by recruiter |

- Conduct a full group discussion about how best to recruit and what to do if someone says no.

## Key Concepts:

- Enthusiasm is your best attitude for effective recruiting.

- Know the job to be done.

- Do your homework.  Know the skills and interests of the people you are trying to recruit and describe why you have asked them.

- Link people with a personal contact within the group quickly.

- Be honest about the job.

- Value the person and the job you asked her to do.

## Sample Discussion Questions:

1.  What qualities are you looking for in a recruiter?

2.  How do you respond if someone says no?

3.  What are your next steps when a person agrees to volunteer?

4.  Who is responsible for recruiting in our organization?

# Principles of Recruiting

1.   The first person to really talk to is yourself!   Discard all the old recruiting techniques.  Be sure that you don't apologize, lie, diminish the job, twist arms or beg.

2.   It is preferable to ask face to face.  Most people volunteer because someone they know asked them.

3.   Be enthusiastic.  Your best recruiter is someone who likes what he/she is doing and values the work of the organization.  Enthusiasm is catching.

4.   Do your homework.  Know the skills, knowledge and attitudes required to do the job.   Prepare a one page job description outlining the purpose of the job, its responsibilities and how to get help.

5.   Go where these skills are found in abundance.  The trend today is to focused recruitment.  Match the right person with the right job.  Don't be satisfied with any "warm body".

6.   Explain why you asked them.  Be explicit about "what's in it for them?"  Try to put yourself in their shoes.  What needs might this job satisfy for volunteers?

It is important to talk openly about volunteers' hopes and dreams.  You may discover additional motivators for volunteering.  For example:

- the student        -        to practise new skills
                     -        to explore a possible future career
                     -        credit course, work at school

- the senior         -        a feeling of being useful and needed
                     -        new friends
                     -        giving back to community

- a young mom        -        a break from the kids
                     -        keeping up work related skills
                     -        developing new skills for the future

- the unemployed -       a sense of self worth
                     -        something for a resumé
                     -        future contacts

7.  Ask!!!  Most people who don't volunteer say it's because no one asked them. Don't apologize for asking people to join you.  Try the following approaches... "I have an opportunity for you......" or  "I've heard so much about your skills....."

8.  Answer their questions.

    Demonstrate your interest in their concerns.  Remember this is the "no surprises" school of volunteer management.  Even if the individual says no to you, you've told the story of your organization.  You may lay the groundwork for future involvement or for a referral to other people.  When you think of recruiting as "friend raising", even a negative response may become a success story.

> **A meaningful task that challenges the volunteer is inherently rewarding.                              - Marlene Wilson**

9.  Link recruits quickly with a specific project and a personal contact.

    Agreeing to help takes courage.  Be sure to get people involved while their interest and enthusiasm are high.  Many people offer to volunteer and then are not contacted.  This really hurts the reputation and credibility of your organization.

    A specific project is the "hook" to get people involved.  They are contributing "on the job", learning the language and culture of your organization.  Don't have them observing for the first year.  These folks will drift away.

> **More volunteers rust out than burnout!**

    A personal contact by a person in authority makes the newcomer feel welcome. Consider assigning a buddy or mentor to watch over a new recruit.  A buddy can make the adjustment to volunteering friendly and easy.

10. Don't Promise What You Can't Deliver

    It may be tempting to offer the world to a hesitant person whom you are trying to recruit.  Resist the temptation.  Promising what you can't deliver makes people resentful and sets up a series of expectations that are not realized.

# Chapter Six

## Making The Right Match

## Title: The Window of Work

*Purpose:*

To identify volunteer interests and skills so that an appropriate volunteer job can be created or assigned.

*When To Use This Exercise:*

If you are meeting with an individual, distribute the form prior to the initial placement interview. Be sure to review it after the completion of a project to update and re-assign the volunteer. It can be used at board and committee meetings as a way to get to know one another better, or at a Nominating Committee to determine Board candidates.

*How Long:*

This exercise should not be done in a single setting but improves when it is reviewed over several periods. One or two hours in total is suggested to ensure that people have sufficient time to explore their interests and share their insights.

*How To Use It:*

- Read the "Window of Work" and "Conducting a Selection Interview" theory in this chapter.

- Pre-circulate the Window of Work and instructions to the volunteer prior to the placement interview, or distribute at an information meeting or orientation.

- Discuss the Window of Work results personally with the volunteer at the interview time, using the information generated to discuss a job that:

   - utilizes one or two skills
   - provides an opportunity in at least one growth area
   - shuns the person's Areas to Avoid

- This process, used in conjunction with the Volunteer Opportunity Book, helps you focus on the volunteer's interests and skills as you look for an appropriate match during an interview or as you assign tasks to committee members.

- At the end of any project, have people "revisit" their windows. Over time, a learning need will become a skill to offer and other areas for growth may be identified.

## *Key Concepts:*

- People work best at tasks they want to do.

- The work itself is by far the most important motivator.

- We don't create motivation, we discover it.

- The best way to know what people are looking for is to ASK them.

## *Sample Questions:*

1. Was this an easy exercise to do?

2. Which section did you find most pleasurable? Most surprising?

3. Does it help you identify the kinds of volunteer projects you might enjoy doing?

4. How might you use this with volunteers in your group?

   - during the interview?

   - after projects are completed?

   - when looking for future leaders?

Be sure to explain how this information will be used. You may want to file these forms in a binder alphabetically so they are available for ready reference, or place them in volunteers' files.

This material is adapted from Ivan Scheier's book, *Staff-Volunteer Relations Collection,* "Building Work That Satisfies, 1: Volunteers and the Window of Work", Energize Inc., 1988.

# Window of Volunteer Work

## Instructions

We are interested in finding a volunteer job for you that will be satisfying, challenging and fun. Prior to our meeting, I would ask you to please complete the Window of Work on the reverse side.

Each of us has a wide range of skills, interests and abilities. We find some tasks more enjoyable and meaningful than others. The obvious conclusion is that you are more likely to be motivated if you <u>want</u> to do the work. This Window of Work helps us focus on your interests, skills and personal growth needs.

On the form you will note:

**Skills to Give:**
- Things you like to do and would willingly offer to do as a volunteer

**Personal Growth Areas:**
- Things you would like to learn
- We will discuss how we might help you enhance the skill(s)

**Areas to Avoid:**
- Things you don't want to do as a volunteer, even though you may have that skill or ability

Think about your own skills and interests, those areas where you would like to build or learn a skill and those things you really don't enjoy or want to do.

In preparing your **Window of Work**, you might choose to work on it for a short while, leave it and then come back to it. Consider asking friends or family to give you advice about what you should list.

Often people find it easier to start with the areas to avoid. We seem more comfortable about listing what we don't enjoy than listing what we think we're good at.

Please consider broadly your interests, skills and talents. Don't limit yourself to a particular job function. Lastly, have fun with this exercise. Your list may surprise you.

We will be discussing the exercise and your results at our meeting. Enjoy!

## The Window of Work

| Skills to Give | Personal Growth Areas | Areas to Avoid |
| --- | --- | --- |
|  |  |  |

Adapted from the work of Ivan Scheier

# Applying the Window of Work

Dr. Ivan Scheier, who created the Window of Work, suggests that the simplest way to find out what people are looking for is to ASK them. Volunteers are more likely to be motivated if they want to do the work. By discussing together the likes and dislikes identified in this process, you are able to focus your interview in a very positive way and better match people with the work to be done. Encouraging people to "open" their windows of work is fun and often an insightful learning experience.

Allow a few moments before the interview starts for the prospective volunteer to browse through the Volunteer Opportunity Book described in Chapter Four. This gives an overview of potential assignments.

At the beginning of the interview, don't rush into making a hasty decision. Take your time and get to know the person. Discuss the interests and skills identified by the volunteer and try to design an appealing job that uses some of those skills and also provides an opportunity to develop at least one growth area. This opportunity for learning is a powerful motivation for people. Try to avoid the things they don't like to do or, at the very least, acknowledge that there may be a few less desirable tasks in an otherwise very desirable job.

Study the following example of a completed Window of Work:

## The Window of Work

**Volunteer Name:** Greg Woodruff                    **Date:** November '93

| Skills to Offer | Personal Growth Areas | Things to Avoid |
|---|---|---|
| • *Great organizational skills*<br><br>• *Like to ask for money*<br><br>• *Get along well with people*<br><br>• *Like to make speeches* | • *Have never chaired a committee*<br><br>• *More formal knowledge about fundraising* | • *Only being given part of a job*<br><br>• *Things where I won't see results*<br><br>• *Stuffing envelopes* |

Should you be fortunate enough to have a person like Greg Woodruff interested in volunteering with your organization, you might discuss the possibility that he be Vice-Chair of the Fundraising Committee and:

a)    have an opportunity to learn meeting management skills from the experienced chair who will be retiring from the board next year;

b)    enrol in a fundraising course for which you might offer to cover half of the tuition costs.

Using a Window of Work will make your interviews more satisfying and productive.

Remember, though, that for each volunteer, interests and areas for growth can and do change over time.  When you provide an opportunity for growth, once the volunteer has mastered that skill it may no longer serve as a motivator.  For this reason, be sure to record the date the Window of Work was completed.

At the end of an assignment, volunteers should be encouraged to update their interests and growth wishes.  Even long term volunteers will enjoy a chance to list their preferences. Discussing talents and growth interests with each other in small groups can be a great focus for a volunteer meeting and help people in your organization or on your committee get to know each other better.

# Title: Forms for Productive Interviews

## *Purpose:*

To enhance people's skill in conducting effective interviews and assist with the initial orientation of volunteers. The Checklist of Interview Tasks and other forms help ensure that you have covered all the key information required to make an appropriate match.

## *When to Use:*

These forms will be completed during an interview with a prospective volunteer.

## *How Long:*

You may ask the prospective volunteer to complete the Information Form prior to coming for the interview. The checklist and other forms are completed when you meet together.

## *How To Use It:*

•   Send the Information Form along with the Window of Work to the prospective volunteer and request that they be completed prior to the interview.

•   During the interview review the information and clarify as required. Should the person decide to volunteer, be sure that all pertinent information has been exchanged and recorded. The Interview Checklist will help here.

•   If the volunteer will be providing transportation or using a car for delivery purposes, you may want to use the forms suggested for drivers. This ensures that you have discussed the key insurance and liability issues.

•   Using a Confidentiality Contract ensures that a discussion of confidentiality occurs during the interview. It is especially important to discuss typical confidentiality issues during orientation sessions for volunteers.

•   These forms should be kept in the volunteer's file.

## *Key Concepts:*

•   Maintaining a good recordkeeping system will assist in the consistent implementation of agency policies and procedures.

•   An organization has the responsibility to be clear about driver liability, confidentiality, reimbursement of expenses and so forth.

## Checklist of Interview Tasks

Name of Person Interviewed: _____

**Prior to Interview**

| | Sent | Received |
|---|---|---|
| Window of Work and letter | ☐ | ☐ |
| Volunteer Information Form | ☐ | ☐ |
| Reference Check(s) | ☐ | ☐ |

Date of Interview: _____

| | Yes | No |
|---|---|---|
| Confidentiality Contract | ☐ | ☐ |
| Driver Insurance Disclosure | ☐ | ☐ |
| Proof of Valid License | ☐ | ☐ |
| Driver Liability Agreement | ☐ | ☐ |
| Policies and Procedures | ☐ | ☐ |
| Reimbursement of Expenses | ☐ | ☐ |
| Orientation Kit Provided | ☐ | ☐ |
| Additional Materials | ☐ | ☐ |
| Uniform Provided | ☐ | ☐ |

Signature: _____

**Placement Decided** _____  **Position:** _____

**Post Interview Tasks**

Reference Check(s) ☐
Welcome Package ☐
Assignment of Buddy/Mentor ☐ Name: _____

Orientation 1

Date: _____

Orientation 2

Date: _____

Training Proposed: _____

---

## Sample Volunteer Information Form

Name: _____  Telephone:(h) _____

Address: _____  Telephone:(b) _____

1. How did you hear about our organization?

2. Have you been involved with other volunteer services in the community?
   Yes ☐   No ☐   If yes, please describe:

3. Describe your main reasons for wishing to volunteer.

4. Can you commit your services for:

   a minimum of three months        Yes ☐  No ☐
   two to four hours/week           Yes ☐  No ☐
   once in a while only             Yes ☐  No ☐

5. Do you prefer to volunteer during:

   Mornings ☐   Afternoons ☐   Evenings ☐
   Mon. ☐  Tues. ☐  Wed. ☐  Thurs. ☐  Fri. ☐  Sat. ☐  Sun. ☐

6. References: (Other than family members)

   Name: _____
   Address: _____
   Telephone: _____
   Relationship to Applicant _____

   Name: _____
   Address: _____
   Telephone: _____
   Relationship to Applicant _____

   I give my permission to contact the above references in regard to my application to volunteer.

   _____
   Signature

Thank you for completing the above. You will be contacted to arrange for a personal interview and further discuss your areas of interest. We appreciate your interest and support!

## Sample Volunteer Contract

**Confidentiality:**

The importance of confidentiality with respect to the people served by our organization and their family, as well as fellow volunteers and staff has been explained to me. I have received a copy of the Volunteer Policies and understand that should I breach this contract of confidentiality I will no longer be able to volunteer with the organization.

**Reliability:**

I understand that as a volunteer I am expected to be dependable and reliable. Should I be unable to fulfil my commitment I will notify the appropriate person promptly.

I understand that to enhance my effectiveness as a volunteer it is expected that I will attend the orientation and training sessions that the organization offers.

Signed:

## Sample Introduction Letter

Dear:

Thank you for enquiring about volunteering. I look forward to meeting you and learning more about how your interests in volunteering might match the needs of our organization.

Enclosed are two forms which we ask you to complete and return to us at your earliest convenience (or bring with you when you come for your interview). The Volunteer Information Form will provide us with background information about your interest in volunteering with us. The "Window of Work" will assist us in placing you in a volunteer position that you will enjoy. Instructions are found on the reverse side of the "Window of Work".

Once we have received this information we will arrange a mutually convenient interview time.

When you come for the interview we will talk about your interests and how they might fit with the volunteer opportunities available. For your information we have enclosed brochures describing our programs and services.

Thanks again for your interest. We look forward to receiving your application information (We look forward to meeting you).

Sincerely,

Contact Person (Title)
Organization

## Sample Driver Liability and Proof of License

Driver Liability:

The importance of having liability insurance on the car I would use to provide transportation for the _____ organization has been explained to me. I understand that I cannot drive unless I have _____ coverage and a valid drivers license.

Volunteer Signature:

Date:

Signature    (attach license to the form and photocopy for the file)

## Sample Volunteer Driver Insurance Disclosure Form

It has been the practice of some insurance companies to require that volunteers complete a disclosure declaration about their intent to be a volunteer driver. It is recommended that you inform volunteer drivers about this issue and advise them to consult with their insurance company. You could provide a copy of this disclosure form to use should it be required.

Your Insurance Company
Address

To Whom It May Concern:

To ensure that my insurance under the policy number noted below is properly effective, I hereby advise you that I am planning to provide my services with an automobile as a volunteer driver for · · · · · · · · · · · ·, a volunteer organization.

I will. . . . . will not. . . . . be receiving mileage compensation for the use of my automobile. I expect to be using my car for this purpose not more than . . . . times per month.

I hereby request any necessary endorsement to my policy to properly provide coverage while using my car for the purpose of a volunteer driver.

Signed:

PLEASE PRINT

Name of Insured:
Name of Insurer:
Policy Number:
Street Address:
City:
Province/State:
Postal Code/ZIP Code:
Telephone:
Contact Person at Organization:
Telephone Number:

# Chapter Seven

## Title: The Coaching PACT

*Purpose:*

To provide a process to enhance people's ability to coach volunteers.

*When To Use This Exercise:*

This exercise is designed to help leadership volunteers and/or staff think through the process of coaching. It is appropriate for:

•    people who agree to take a leadership position with your organization
•    those who chair committees
•    new staff, as part of their orientation to working successfully with volunteers

*How Long?*

Allow an hour and a half for this exercise.

*How To Use It:*

•    Read the theory handout "Coaching: Learning to Empower Others".

•    Begin with a brief discussion of the changing role of supervision, especially in the voluntary sector. Highlight the value of a supervisory style that encourages people to work independently, with increasing freedom to make decisions and take action.

    Working in groups of three or four, ask participants to identify the trends and expectations that suggest the need for a different relationship between volunteers and staff. Allow about ten minutes for this discussion, giving people just enough time to feel comfortable with one another. Together, list their results on the flipchart paper. They will identify items similar to those listed on page 73.

•    Display on an overhead or flipchart, "What Do Effective Coaches Do?".

•    A novel approach to demonstrating effective coaching is to use "Sister Act", a popular video. In this video, Whoopi Goldberg coaches a choir of earnest but ineffective nuns. The clip to use focuses on Whoopi's intervention with the choir.

    Before showing the clip, ask participants to carefully watch the "coach's" approach and be prepared to talk about it. Lead a full group discussion about what the coach did. Page 73 of the theory suggests answers you might expect.

- Summarize the full group discussion with some of the more widely held ideas about what skills make for effective coaching. Refer to "The Coaching PACT".

- Introduce the PACT Coaching Sheet which outlines the four components of the model: Purpose, Activities, Concepts and Tomorrow. Reproduce the form on page 67.

- Work in small groups to apply the PACT model to typical coaching scenarios, using one of the suggested samples or developing others that are of pressing interest to your agency. People will need 25 minutes to handle the scenarios and summarize their discussion on flipchart paper.

- Have each group report back on their discussions, outlining their responses using the PACT model. Each group will need 8 - 10 minutes to report back and field questions from the full group. There are many possible right answers to each scenario.

- Conclude the session by having people talk in pairs about what they have learned and how they can apply this process in their support of volunteers.

### Key Concepts:

- The coaching process provides an opportunity for staff or leadership volunteers to learn while carrying out their volunteer assignment.

- Coaching is not telling people what to do but helping them make decisions and take action.

- Coaching uses a variety of techniques, tailored to the need of the volunteer and the situation under discussion.

- By planning your coaching intervention, you can offer broader and more thoughtful support to volunteers.

- There are many possible approaches to coaching but the principles remain the same. The volunteer is able to choose those strategies that best fit his/her needs.

### Sample Questions:

1. What do effective coaches do? What is their relationship with volunteers?

2. In your opinion, why are staff and leadership volunteers reluctant to act as coaches, preferring to behave in the more traditional role as supervisor?

3. What skills must we develop to be more effective as coaches?

4. How might we use this process and form in our organization? What revisions might we like to see included?

# The Coaching PACT
Purpose - Activities - Concepts - Tomorrow

**1.** **PURPOSE** of this intervention:

**2.** **ACTIVITIES** most appropriate for this situation:

☐ Listening
☐ Clarifying, Restating
☐ Building trust (attending)
☐ Posing alternatives
☐ Reflecting other points of view
☐ Facilitating the exchange of resources
 ☐ Person power
 ☐ Money ☐ Equipment
 ☐ Tools/techniques ☐ Knowledge
☐ Delegating
☐ Problem solving
☐ Conflict resolution
☐ Training (1:1)

Strategies:

**3.** Key **CONCEPTS** to be communicated:

**4.** **TOMORROW**

☐ Systems and supports to strengthen this volunteer:

☐ Improvements that will benefit other volunteers:

# Coaching Scenarios

### Scenario #1

Suzanne is a new Big Sister. She telephones you, obviously very upset. Her little sister, Tamela, has stolen fifty dollars from Suzanne's purse. Feeling sick about the situation, Suzanne didn't even confront Tamela at the time. This incident has really put a cramp in their relationship. Suzanne doesn't know how to proceed.

Your organization has a policy about reporting stolen property. Suzanne is expected to write an incident report. Even more important, she is expected to resolve the incident with Tamela in a helpful manner. She must encourage respect for private property and articulate her disapproval of Tamela's behaviour. At the same time she must demonstrate acceptance of Tamela as a worthwhile and loved person.

### Scenario #2

Marlene is the Chair of the Fundraising Committee in your organization. She comes to you feeling very discouraged about the commitment of committee members to get out and raise money as well as her ability as chair. People are not willing to take responsibility for acting on decisions made but prefer to leave the work to her. There is poor attendance at meetings and those who come lack energy or enthusiasm.

### Scenario #3

Wendy has just called to report that Mr. Cameron, the elderly gentleman she has been visiting for almost two years, has died. Wendy is weepy over the phone and keeps repeating "I just didn't see it coming. It's such a shock. I feel like I have lost my own father." You invite Wendy to come right over to see you.

### Scenario #4

Joseph is about to visit a nearby public school to speak on behalf of your agency for the very first time. He pops into your office, full of misgivings and doubts about the actual event. He seems to have forgotten everything you taught him in the presentation workshop he attended last year.

## The Coaching PACT
### Purpose - Activities - Concepts - Tomorrow

*Scenario #1*

**1. PURPOSE of this intervention:**
demonstrate my confidence in her
familiarize with policy
encourage a workable solution
identify next steps - Complete INCIDENT report

**3. Key CONCEPTS to be communicated:**
- She can handle this.
- This is an opportunity to build relationship
- Her role is to build values.
   Don't Solve It for Her!

**2. ACTIVITIES most appropriate for this situation:**
- ☑ Listening
- ☑ Clarifying, Restating
- ☑ Building trust (attending)
- ☑ Posing alternatives    Tamela's viewpoint
- ☑ Reflecting other points of view
- ☐ Facilitating the exchange of resources
   - ☐ Person power    ☐ Equipment
   - ☐ Money    ☑ Knowledge
   - ☐ Tools/techniques    · POLICY Book
- ☐ Delegating
- ☑ Problem solving
- ☑ Conflict resolution
- ☐ Training (1:1)

Strategies:
· Press for full account
· Acknowledge her feelings of upset.
· Find out Tamela's views
① Listen to her account.
② Determine what has been done.
③ Encourage policy check.
④ Clarify next steps - Role Play?
   Suzanne's goals with Tamela
⑤ Complete Incident Report

**4. TOMORROW**

☐ Systems and supports to strengthen this volunteer:
Role play - Suzanne - I'll be Tamela. Try out her approach.
Check back on results - by March 15

☐ Improvements that will benefit other volunteers:
Is this a topic for next volunteer inservice?
· Breaches of Trust
· Building Values
· Coaching Kids.

---

## The Coaching PACT
### Purpose - Activities - Concepts - Tomorrow

*Scenario #2*

**1. PURPOSE of this intervention:**
enhance Marlene's ability to chair
build her skill, problem solve, offer resources, listen to her frustration
hear what's been tried

**3. Key CONCEPTS to be communicated:**
· notion of group development, stages
· involvement = ↑ participation
· role of chair to involve not SOLVE
· confidence in her    · need to review

**2. ACTIVITIES most appropriate for this situation:**
- ☑ Listening
- ☑ Clarifying, Restating
- ☑ Building trust (attending)
- ☑ Posing alternatives
- ☑ Reflecting other points of view - Committee members
- ☐ Facilitating the exchange of resources
   - ☑ Person power Bob    ☐ Equipment
   - ☐ Money    ☑ Knowledge
   - ☑ Tools/techniques    Great book Group Gold
- ☐ Delegating
- ☑ Problem solving
- ☐ Conflict resolution    Process check
- ☑ Training (1:1)

Strategies:
1. Listen to full picture
2. What has she tried?
3. Group stage - what is expected
4. What else might she try - her ideas
5. Direct to Bob, excellent CHAIRING skills

**4. TOMORROW**

☐ Systems and supports to strengthen this volunteer:
① Attend next meeting with Marlene pre-plan ⟶ de-brief, VIDEO?
② Set up follow up DATE to review
③ Share article on Group Development
④ Results of Process Check - see EVALUATIONS - discuss

☐ Improvements that will benefit other volunteers:
· All new chairs would benefit from start up training
· Build in tips for INVOLVING silent members

---

---

**Scenario #3**

## The Coaching PACT
### Purpose - Activities - Concepts - Tomorrow

**1. PURPOSE of this intervention:**

offer support, comfort

? assess readiness for new client

**3. Key CONCEPTS to be communicated:**

- Grief normal - Expected
- Wendy's intervention was helpful, important
- others understand + accept her
- resources to help her understand - will not lessen PAIN.

**2. ACTIVITIES most appropriate for this situation:**

- ☑ Listening
- ☐ Clarifying, Restating
- ☑ Building trust (attending) *Share grief*
- ☐ Posing alternatives
- ☐ Reflecting other points of view
- ☐ Facilitating the exchange of resources
  - ☑ Person power   ☐ Equipment
  - ☐ Money          ☑ Knowledge
  - ☐ Tools/techniques
- ☐ Delegating
- ☐ Problem solving
- ☐ Conflict resolution
- ☐ Training (1:1)

*Talk to Megan.*
*• Similar experience last month*
*Great Book - On Death + Dying Kubhler-Ross*

Strategies:
1. Listen, Listen, Listen
2. Relaxed atmosphere ↓ intrusions Kleenex, make tea
3. Encourage her to talk about positive experiences
4. Acknowledge GRIEF painful - Share story
5. Check on her PLANS - talk with Megan

**4. TOMORROW**

☐ Systems and supports to strengthen this volunteer:

- Call next week - Aug. 20 to check
- Re-assign with care - ? more positive outcome
- Encourage link with Megan

☐ Improvements that will benefit other volunteers:

- Inservice on grieving -
- More open discussion on preparing to terminate a relationship
- ? Buddies

---

**Scenario #4**

## The Coaching PACT
### Purpose - Activities - Concepts - Tomorrow

**1. PURPOSE of this intervention:**

Build confidence
Rehearse
Ensure accuracy + competence
? Provide backup.

**3. Key CONCEPTS to be communicated:**

- he can do it well
- represents our agency
- he can say he doesn't know answer
- my commitment to his success

**2. ACTIVITIES most appropriate for this situation:**

- ☑ Listening
- ☐ Clarifying, Restating
- ☐ Building trust (attending)
- ☑ Posing alternatives
- ☐ Reflecting other points of view
- ☐ Facilitating the exchange of resources
  - ☑ Person power   ☐ Equipment
  - ☐ Money          ☐ Knowledge
  - ☑ Tools/techniques
- ☐ Delegating
- ☐ Problem solving
- ☐ Conflict resolution
- ☑ Training (1:1)

*Does he need an experienced presenter with him?*
*CHECKLIST - create it STEP by STEP together*

Strategies:
1. Identify mixed feelings · excitement → fear
2. Outline PLANS - checklist
3. Answer questions
4. Pose typical hitches - if AV fails difficult questions
5. Offer experienced SUPPORT

**4. TOMORROW**

☐ Systems and supports to strengthen this volunteer:

Compliment PLANS -
Confidence in him "I like what you've suggested."

Call Jeff about possible backup.
Contact June 30 re outcome

☐ Improvements that will benefit other volunteers:

- Should checklist be part of our Training Package?
- How about Buddies first time out?
- Possible rehearsal for facility staff before real world assignment.

---

## How to Use the Coaching PACT
Purpose - Activities - Concepts - Tomorrow

This form is designed to help staff and leadership volunteers plan a coaching intervention with a volunteer who needs help. The specific help needed will be different in each situation. Let's look at each component of the PACT form:

**Purpose** of this intervention:

The coach identifies what she is trying to do. There may be several purposes at play at the same time. Some are unclear as you plan but may develop during the interaction itself. For example, in Scenario 3, is Wendy ready for another client match or would that seem insensitive? Remember, the role of the coach is not to DO - to solve the problem, to resolve the conflict or to answer all of the questions. Rather, it is to "enable" the volunteer to do it.

**Activities** most appropriate for this situation:

The PACT form lists coaching behaviours, with space for you to briefly note your potential responses for any activity. See the sample PACT forms illustrated in this chapter.

**Listening:** The bedrock of coaching, listening is part of every intervention. You are listening for content, feelings, unanswered questions and confusion.

**Clarifying:** The coach asks clarifying questions to ensure he understands what has been said. These additional questions may bring new insights to the volunteer.

**Building trust:** What can the coach do to demonstrate acceptance of the volunteer's feelings and confidence in the volunteer's ability to successfully complete the task?

**Posing alternatives:** The successful coach helps the volunteer broaden potential responses to any situation. Rather than becoming stuck with a single position, he asks "If we did this, what would happen?" By exploring a range of options, the coach helps the volunteer select the best possible response to the situation.

**Reflecting other points of view:** The coach encourages the volunteer to consider the opinions, feelings and perspective of others involved. "I wonder how Tamela views this event?" might be a question posed in Scenario 1. This gives the volunteer all the needed data to make a wise decision to proceed.

**Facilitating the exchange of resources:** Can the coach direct the volunteer to someone who has wrestled with a similar problem? What tools or techniques might be used to influence the desired results? Is there equipment or technology that might be useful? For example, might we videotape the next committee meeting in Scenario 2 for review by Marlene and the coach? Knowledge might include where to find information -a policy book, an article in a professional journal, a video on training.

**Delegating:** Assigning a project or problem to a volunteer for action. The coach may initiate the interaction, clarifying what needs to be done, under what conditions and by what date. Much of the difficulty in effective delegation comes from the failure to CLEARLY outline the desired results.

**Problem Solving:** Is the problem statement clear and complete? Do we have all the data we need to suggest alternatives? Are all possible solutions explored? Are criteria set for selecting a solution? Are concrete action steps outlined? Is responsibility assigned? Is a date for evaluation in place?

**Conflict Resolution:** What is the issue? What need does it attempt to address? What does the other party in the conflict want or need? What are the barriers to resolution? Can they be accommodated? What other options exist? How might these be most successfully presented?

**Training:** Is there a gap in knowledge, skill or attitude that can be filled with some training? How might this be accomplished?

**Strategies:** The volunteer with the help of the coach outlines a step-by-step approach to implement the selected activities, listing possible alternatives. Creating a sequential action plan is helpful.

Key **Concepts** to be communicated: The most important ideas you want to share with the volunteer. Keep the concept list short to ensure understanding and retention.

**Tomorrow**:

**Systems and supports that will strengthen this volunteer:**

This section focuses on making sure the results of the coaching session are acted upon and that the volunteer has the help needed to apply the concepts successfully. Examples of future supports would be assigning a buddy, a follow-up phone call, a note to congratulate the volunteer.

**Improvements that will benefit other volunteers:**

In offering support to an individual, a coach often identifies a resource that would be helpful for all volunteers. She might also note a gap in current practice that could be remedied. For example, offering an inservice training on grieving would be useful for all Friendly Visitors in Scenario 3.

# Coaching: Learning to Empower Others

The management of human resources today cries out for a different approach, a new relationship between supervisor/manager and the person being supervised. In the more traditional, hierarchial model, the supervisor makes decisions and directs the work of "his" staff. This top down approach just doesn't fit the needs or skills of today's workers. They are anxious to be part of the decision making that affects them. Rather than concentrating on controlling people, managers are now urged to put in place systems that support risk taking and innovation. The role of leadership is to empower all people. Empowerment encourages volunteers to take increasing measures of responsibility for their own actions and increasing involvement in the decisions that affect them.

Trends in volunteer expectations suggest the need for a different relationship between supervisors and staff or volunteers that is characterized by:

* more professional approach to mobilizing volunteers
* broader role in decision making
* better educated workforce who wants to be consulted
* volunteer group with professional skills to offer
* expectation to enjoy their work and make a difference
* more selective willingness to help
* acknowledgement that their needs are respected
* chance to be creative and to approach a task as they see fit.

## What Do Effective Coaches Do?

* enhance the competence and confidence of each team member
* support efforts
* build and maintain positive working relationships
* clarify goals and objectives
* remove obstacles to achievement of goals
* offer training (mostly on the job)

The actions that one observes in successful coaches include setting standards, clarifying mission, unifying actions, creating alliances, respecting past traditions, listening, rewarding positive behaviours and setting the task in the frame of reference of team. The skills that make for effective coaching are discussed in the accompanying handout, The Coaching PACT.

To change attitude and encourage the adoption of coaching behaviour, volunteers need a chance to look at their attitudes and talk through the risks of change. We are asking volunteers to behave in very new ways. In these circumstances it is easy to feel both threatened and under-appreciated. This vulnerability is a cue for the trainer to be available to those testing out new ways of behaving and to be ready to acknowledge positive behaviours, in other words, to be a coach.

*The Leadership Challenge* by Kouzes and Posner is a helpful resource in understanding the emerging leadership role that a coach enjoys. It identifies five practices of exemplary leaders, and describes strategies for strengthening others. Exemplary leaders share power widely. The more employees believe they can influence and control the organization, the greater the organizational effectiveness. Rosabeth Moss Kanter, the respected editor of Harvard Business Review, identifies four principles to strengthen others by giving people:

- **important work** to do on **critical** issues.
- **discretion** and **autonomy** over their tasks and resources
- **visibility** to others and provide **recognition** for effort
- opportunities to connect with powerful people, finding them **sponsors** and **mentors**.

One additional principle is critical. Give people information. The author William Bridges claims that for every week you withhold information, you suffer six months of mistrust. Sharing both good and bad news regularly and with candour does much to eliminate the "we-they" of boss and team members.

How can we empower volunteers and staff in our organizations? It is crucial to ask ourselves some tough questions:

What are real examples of important work to be done?
How could we integrate volunteers?
What current practices suggest we don't trust staff or volunteers?
What current behaviours of managers suggest that only supervisors can think or plan?
What information is currently withheld?

Once we identify practises and policies that "dis-able", we can put in place initiatives that permit a new climate of openness and innovation.

# Chapter Eight

## Title: The Volunteer Self Assessment Tool

### *Purpose:*

To encourage the development of a positive attitude about evaluation. To create a practice within the organization of using evaluation to:

*   acknowledge work well done;
*   identify growth by the volunteer;
*   plot out with a supportive person, the future involvement for that volunteer.

### *When to Use This Exercise:*

Volunteer evaluation is a topic that remains controversial. Although the benefits to both the volunteer and the organization can be clearly demonstrated, many people feel uncomfortable about having their efforts judged. Introducing a self-assessment process is a less threatening approach. In implementing this process, consider initially working with:

*   those who express an interest in having formal feedback about their performance.
*   new volunteers introduced to the self evaluation process as part of their orientation.
*   current volunteers when staff performance review is introduced.

It is probably best is not to press the issue. Let the successes of others be the prompt to encourage volunteers who are uncomfortable or uncertain. This form can be discussed after a presentation on the Volunteer Assignment Outline.

### *How Long?*

Allow about an hour and a half for this exercise.

### *How to Use It:*

*   Read the accompanying theory handouts on Volunteer Evaluation. Reproduce copies of the Volunteer Assessment Form on page 78 by enlarging it.

*   Begin by putting the word **evaluation** on the board and asking people to give you their immediate response to it. You will get both positive and negative responses. Acknowledge the discomfort some people feel about being evaluated.

- Have the group identify the benefits of evaluation for the organization and the individual. If you sense some hesitation to speak up in the full group, invite participants to discuss the issue for a few minutes in groups of three. Record their responses on flipchart paper.

- Break into small groups. Ask people to talk about an experience with evaluation that was positive and where they learned more about themselves. The group will need twenty minutes to discuss this topic. Ask each group to create **Guidelines for Effective Evaluation** based on their own experience and to post their results on flipchart paper.

- Invite participants to circulate around the room, reading other groups' responses. Hold a full group discussion to develop a complete list, using the sample discussion questions on the next page to identify all the key concepts. To reinforce these concepts, use an overhead of "Guidelines for Evaluating Volunteer Performance" in this section.

- Distribute the copies of the Assessment Form (label it **DRAFT**). Describe how it has been designed with special emphasis on the success measures. If this topic has not been covered in the job design segment of your training, you will need to discuss that now. Outline the suggested process for carrying out an assessment. You might prepare an overhead of "The Performance Review Process".

- Refer to an existing volunteer assignment that you believe most people will understand and identify what a self assessment might look like. See sample forms and instructions for suggestions.

- Encourage suggestions to make the form more appropriate for your own agency. An opportunity to change the form and comment on the process will increase their willingness to participate in a trial of the proposed self-assessment process.

### Key Concepts:

- Evaluation is designed to help people feel good about the work they do, achieve organizational goals, and repeat good work.

- Increasingly volunteers are asking for feedback about performance.

- When a position description outlines success measures, the volunteer has a clear picture of what is expected.

- Performance problems must be immediately addressed, not at a project's end.

- Failure to meet success measures may be a staff responsibility, not a volunteer issue.

- The Guidelines for Evaluating Volunteer Performance should be followed.

- The Performance Review Process is a suggested process only. Each organization is encouraged to adapt the process to meet its needs. Volunteers should be given an opportunity to provide input on improving the process.

### Sample Questions:

- In your opinion, why do people feel uncomfortable about evaluation?

- What might a staff person or volunteer leader do to reduce the sense of discomfort of someone coming to discuss a self evaluation with them?

- If someone failed to reach his/her success measures, what would be a helpful response from the staff or senior volunteer?

- How could we use this form in our agency? What changes in the form or in the process do you recommend?

## Volunteer Self-Assessment Tool (Cont'd)

What aspect of this volunteer assignment did I enjoy?

What would I do differently if I were doing this work again?

What additional support from my liaison/contact would have been helpful?

Would I be willing to carry on with this assignment?

☐ Yes　　　☐ No　　　☐ Would like to discuss

Are there other assignments that I would prefer? Please list here:

Scheduled meeting with contact: (date completed)

## Volunteer Self-Assessment Tool

Name:
Assignment Title:　　Date:
　　Dates Position Held:

Purpose:

Job Responsibilities:

Success Measures:　　Completion Date

1.

2.

3.

4.

5.

Comments:

In completing these responsibilities, I would rank my performance as:

Comments:
☐ Superior, exceeded goal
☐ Excellent job, met goal
☐ Could benefit from further training/assistance

## Volunteer Assignment

| | |
|---|---|
| **Title:** | *Youth Volunteer Basketball Coordinator* |
| **Purpose:** | *To plan and implement a weekly basketball league for boys and girls ages 10-16.* |
| **Job Responsibilities:** | *1. Draws up schedule for basketball teams.*<br>*2. Ensures that all necessary equipment is available.*<br>*3. Assigns referees and senior volunteer observers.*<br>*4. Reports accidents, injury damage and disturbances.*<br>*5. Identifies outstanding players for MVP awards.* |
| **Skills, Attitudes, Knowledge:** | *• love of basketball*<br>*• good organizational skills*<br>*• commitment, follow-through, responsible to attend weekly*<br>*• enjoys working with youth*<br>*• communication and problem-solving skills* |
| **Relationships/ Liaison:** | *• Reports to Senior Program Staff-Youth on duty* |
| **Time Commitment:**<br>**# Hours:**<br>**Term:**<br>**Peak Time:** | *Games: Thursdays 4:30 - 6:30 (must be present)*<br>*2-3 hours per month planning/communicating*<br>*1 hour per week reporting/recording* |
| **Benefits and Challenges:** | *• First time we've had this position*<br>*• Free membership to Youth Program Leaders Club*<br>*• Letter of reference available upon request*<br>*• Builds leadership/problem solving skills* |
| **Success Measures:** | *• All matches are posted 2 weeks before game*<br>*• All equipment safely maintained and available at start of each game*<br>*• All critical incident reports are filed on the day of incident* |
| **Training:** | *• MVP awards are given to 2 participants each session*<br>*• Level 1 Coaching*<br>*• Leadership training* |

## Volunteer Self-Assessment Tool

**Name:** *Jack Shubert*  **Date:** *Sept. '93*
**Assignment Title:** *Youth Volunteeer Basketball Coordinator*
**Dates Position Held:** *9 months - February '93*

**Purpose:** *To plan and implement a weekly basketball league for boys and girls ages 10 - 16*

**Job Responsibilities:**

*(As outlined in Assignment Outline)*

| Success Measures: | Completion Date |
|---|---|
| 1. *All matches were posted 2 weeks before game* | *Feb. 93 - present* |
| 2. *All equipment available for games* | *✓* |
| 3. *6 critical events reported - all within 24 hours of events* | |
| 4. *2 boys selected for MVP* | *Sept. '93* |
| 5. | |

**Comments:**

*- 2 basketballs stolen - 2 additional balls purchased.*
*- No girls signed up for basketball this term*

**In completing these responsibilities, I would rank my performance as:**

Comments:
- ☑ Superior, exceeded goal
- ☐ Excellent job, met goal
- ☐ Could benefit from further training/assistance

*(Staff supervisor suggested Superior)*

## Volunteer Self-Assessment Tool (Cont'd)

**What aspect of this volunteer assignment did I enjoy?**

- *Making up assignments*
- *Being at games*
  *(didn't like dealing with critical incidents)*

**What would I do differently if I were doing this work again?**

- *Always assign back-up volunteers*
- *Appoint 1 member of team as liaison (I got lots of phone calls/complaints)*
- *Get more girls involved*

**What additional support from my liaison/contact would have been helpful?**

*He was great!*

**Would I be willing to carry on with this assignment?**

☑ Yes          ☐ No          ☐ Would like to discuss

**Are there other assignments that I would prefer? Please list here:**

*Would like to coach Indoor Soccer if possible at some time.*

**Scheduled meeting with contact: (date completed)**

*Met with Supervisior, Sept. '93*

# Volunteer Evaluation:  A Positive Look at Performance Review

Filed in almost everyone's memory bank is the recollection of a personal evaluation that went wrong - you felt attacked as an individual, your competence was questioned, your self-confidence dealt a staggering blow.  Is it any wonder that even the mention of "evaluation" conjures up a negative image?

The purpose of a performance review is not to punish or penalize, but a positive way to acknowledge work well done, identify growth by the volunteer and plot out the future involvement for that volunteer with a supportive person.

In this context, evaluation becomes an affirming event, not one to be feared, avoided or ignored.  It was Ken Blanchard in his book, *The One Minute Manager*, who suggested that the true role of the manager is to find people doing something right and to praise them for it.  As a result good work is repeated and employees feel positive about their performance and contribution to achieving the desired results.

Why is volunteer evaluation becoming a "hot topic"?  There are several factors:

- volunteers themselves are asking "Am I doing a good job?"  They want clear guidelines about what is expected and how they are doing;

- volunteer departments are being more professionally managed.  The volunteer coordinator is asking, "Am I adequately preparing volunteers to do their work within the agency?"  As programs and procedures are evaluated, performance also comes under scrutiny;

- staff performance is being rigorously monitored in a tight economy.  Employers are asking, "How can we maximize the benefits we receive from orientation, training and implementation of new systems and strategies?"  In the voluntary sector, much staff time and talent is spent supervising volunteers.  Is it time well spent?  The only way to know for sure is to monitor the **results** of training and supervision, the behaviour of volunteers.

## Where to Start?

In initiating a Volunteer Performance Review, the best advice is to go SLOWLY to build volunteer buy-in and support.  Set a climate that encourages self-evaluation by initially working with new volunteers and those who are interested in a self-assessment opportunity.  Don't force it on those who are reluctant or resistant.  They may be prepared to join you later when they see the benefits enjoyed by others.

Evaluation starts with the creation of a volunteer assignment which clearly identifies the measures for success.  Success measures are tangible, concrete measures of results.  The volunteer can say with certainty "Yes, I've done that!" Each measure must clearly define what is expected, reflecting the most important aspects of the job.  Let's explore examples of two typical volunteer assignments:

---

### The Canvasser

| Responsibilities | Success Measures |
|---|---|
| 1. Pick up canvasser's kit. | 1. Kit picked up by (date). |
| 2. Visit every home assigned. | 2. Assigned homes visited/envelope left. |
| 3. Call back at least once if no response. | 3. Receipt book complete/accurate. |
| 4. Leave envelope at the door. | 4. Monies and receipt book consistent. |
| 5. Complete official receipt. | 5. Completed canvass materials |
| 6. Tally and return all monies, receipt books to team captain. | 6. Returned by (date). |

### The President

| Responsibilities | Success Measures |
|---|---|
| 1. Initiates annual planning. | 1. Annual plan is in place by (date). |
| 2. Chairs meetings of the Board. | 2. Holds monthly meetings of Board. |
| 3. Ensures adherence to all policies. | 3. Agenda pre-circulated 10 days in advance. |
| 4. Represents the organization locally. | 4. Concerns are addressed within 24 hours. |
| 5. Works with staff to handle problems. | 5. Full slate of officers is in place. |
| 6. Ensures smooth functioning of all organizational committees. | |

---

Success measures for repetitive or simple jobs may be pre-established with little variation permitted. For most jobs, however, you will want to negotiate the Success Measures with each individual. What you expect may vary depending on the experience of that person and the special needs of the organization at any given time. Once the volunteer assignment accurately reflects expectations, then evaluation becomes simpler.

**Not all success measures will be achieved.** Reasons beyond the control of the volunteer may hamper successful completion. Explòre whether performance was hampered by:

- inadequate staff support
- failure to provide the necessary tools to complete the job
- poor matching of volunteer skill to the task assigned
- unrealistic time expectations

These factors indicate the need for a different approach by staff in preparing this volunteer to carry out her assignment. The volunteer coordinator can make the changes with a sense of confidence that future performance will improve.

---

## The Performance Review Process

1. Towards the end of a project the volunteer receives a Self-Assessment Tool for completion.

2. The volunteer is invited to share it with her staff contact or leadership volunteer.

3. The liaison does not complete a form, but comes to the meeting prepared to offer advice, support and to take appropriate action. It is critical to focus on the positives and not use this encounter to berate, correct or discipline the volunteer. Correction is most appropriate during the activity itself when change is possible, not at the end when nothing can be done.

4. The volunteer commits to do the assignment again or to try something different. Together they consider any new success measures and set personal goals for the next year.

5. The Performance Review may become part of the volunteer's record file if the volunteer agrees or can be withheld at the volunteer's request.

## Guidelines for Evaluating Volunteer Performance

Evaluation is based on stated and shared success measures with no surprises or hidden agendas.

Evaluation is based on achievement of the success measures and not on personality or new responsibilities.

The volunteer knows and understands the success measures before the project starts.

The volunteer's perspective is always sought.

The volunteer has an opportunity to evaluate the support provided by his liaison in the setting and achievement of goals.

The volunteer is only held responsible for things he can control. For example, he cannot complete budgets on time if budget forms are not distributed to him; he cannot be criticized for failing to recruit five new members if he has followed proper procedures, made the necessary overtures, but was turned down.

# Chapter Nine

## Title: Successful Volunteer Recognition

### Purpose:

To assist in planning for effective volunteer recognition. This exercise will identify a variety of ways in which volunteers can be recognized and will encourage the development of a year round plan.

### When To Use:

This exercise can be part of a volunteer meeting in late spring or early fall. Following this activity, an advisory group of volunteers and staff can brainstorm additional ideas and organize a plan of action.

### How Long?

Allow about one hour for this exercise.

### How to Use:

- Read the background theory on Recognition. Make an overhead transparency of the Recognition Cycle.

- Start the meeting with a few comments about the importance of recognition. If you used the Motivational Analysis at an earlier meeting, refer to the results of that discussion.

- Ask groups of 3 - 4 to share with each other the recognition they remember as being most meaningful and why. Allow eight to ten minutes for this discussion. Encourage candid feedback about the kinds of recognition people prefer.

- Facilitate a group discussion about the principles of effective recognition and the importance of planning both formal and informal ways of saying thank you.

- Using the overhead of the Volunteer Recognition Cycle, emphasize the importance of informal recognition throughout the year and throughout the volunteer's involvement with your organization.

- Distribute the Volunteer Recognition Worksheet to participants.

- Break into small groups to brainstorm recognition ideas for one or more of the identified categories. If it is a small group you could ask half of them to focus on informal recognition and the other half on formal. Allow 15 minutes for the discussion and a further five minutes to post key ideas on flipchart paper.

- Share the highlights either by reporting verbally from each group or by walking around viewing the summary sheets.

- After the discussion recruit a few participants to help develop a plan for ongoing recognition, using the ideas generated in the session as its foundation.

### Key Concepts:

- To be meaningful and therefore effective, recognition must respond to a person's motivational needs.

- Differing motivational types require different kinds of recognition.

- Recognition should be on ongoing process that happens both formally (public) and informally (personal) throughout the year.

- Creatively appropriate personal recognition is especially effective in sustaining volunteer satisfaction.

- Successful recognition doesn't just happen. It requires thoughtful planning.

- Ongoing support and accurate records are the foundation for successful recognition.

### Sample Discussion Questions:

- What was the most meaningful form of recognition that you remember during your volunteer career? What made it so meaningful?

- What does this discussion tell us about effective recognition?

- How will we ensure that a plan for ongoing recognition is developed and implemented?

- How can we support and recognize the efforts of staff who work well with volunteers?

## Volunteer Recognition Worksheet

| Time | Forms of Recognition | |
| --- | --- | --- |
| | Informal Recognition | Formal Recognition |
| When a volunteer first starts and also when a volunteer leaves | • <br> • <br> • <br> • | • <br> • <br> • <br> • |
| On a regular basis during volunteer's involvement (weekly, monthly) | • <br> • <br> • <br> • | • <br> • <br> • <br> • |
| Annually | • <br> • <br> • <br> • | • <br> • <br> • <br> • |
| On special occasions in the volunteer's life or the calendar year <br><br> After successful assignments | • <br> • <br> • <br> • | • <br> • <br> • <br> • |
| Ways to recognize staff who work well with volunteers | • <br> • <br> • <br> • | • <br> • <br> • <br> • |

| Motivational Type | Recognition |
|---|---|
| **Achievement-Oriented**<br><br>Goal: Success in a situation that requires excellent or improved performance. | • Appreciates pins, certificates<br>• Letters of recommendation to the boss<br>• Name mentioned re: achievement of a specific goal<br>• Promotions - increasing challenges<br>• Training to improve performance<br>• Efficient meetings<br>• Letter from the President<br>• Knowing results<br>• Evaluating the results for improvement |
| **Affiliation-Oriented**<br><br>Goal: To be with others and enjoy mutual friendships. | • Enjoys sharing success with others<br>• Likes to have family and friends included<br>• Feels a project is successful if friendships have developed<br>• Would highly value compliments from a supervisor - personal thank you note, pins or engraved plaque<br>• Would feel personally slighted if not recognized<br>• A great party would be an appropriate acknowledgement |
| **Power-Oriented**<br><br>Goal: To have an impact or influence on others. To bring about social change. | • Public recognition<br>• Opportunity to meet others with power<br>• Media recognition, locally or nationally<br>• Being part of the action<br>• Titles that confer status<br>• Opportunity to innovate<br>• Work with government; play advocacy role |

# Recognition - A Year Round Process

**Effective volunteer recognition requires:**

*   understanding why people volunteer

*   developing a plan to say thanks on an ongoing basis throughout the year

*   delegating a person(s) to be responsible to see that recognition happens

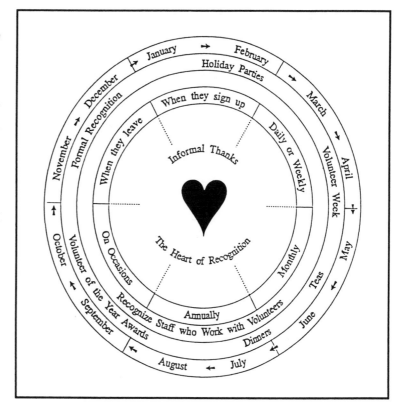

## Who should be responsible for developing and implementing a recognition plan?

In the past, the president of a group often assumed responsibility for supporting and recognizing other volunteers, although this adds to what is usually a significant workload.

Recognition is an excellent activity for the Volunteer Development Committee. A small sub-group of interested volunteers would develop an annual plan for the committee's approval. Specific tasks related to that plan could be delegated to share the load and ensure follow-through. It may be helpful to include a relatively new volunteer to bring a different perspective to your planning.

# Principles of Recognition

✓ Build in **formal** and **informal** ways of saying thanks. While public events enhance visibility in the community and raise awareness of the importance of volunteers to the organization's mission, informal recognition has significant personal impact and keeps people motivated in the longer term.

✓ Be sure that the recognition is **appropriate to a person's needs**.

**User Friendly** recognition reflects an understanding that what may be perceived as positive by one person, may be very uncomfortable for another. Asking a volunteer to give a speech at an annual meeting may be a reward for one and sheer punishment for another!

**Personalized** recognition is based on the notion that people are different, and have different needs and different preferences. Volunteers want to know that you really mean it. No one is thrilled about an invitation to a party that is addressed to the occupant! The old saying, "different strokes for different folks" is absolutely true. Refer back to McClelland's motivational types, in the recognition chart.

Recognition that is **creatively appropriate** will respond most effectively to volunteer needs. Picture a meeting in which a particularly astute volunteer asks tough questions that energize the whole group. The issues needed to be discussed, but you are aware that the person is uncomfortable about other people's reaction. Creatively appropriate recognition should acknowledge the value of that role. Begin the next meeting by presenting that person with a small box of chocolate covered raisins with a note "Thanks for raisin' the tough issues!" This not only supports the volunteer, but it provides an opportunity to discuss together the value of diverse opinions.

Recognition that **meets felt needs** will be most effective. The newly appointed chair of a committee may have indicated a desire to improve her meeting management skills. Providing her with an opportunity to attend a facilitation skills workshop acknowledges the importance of her role and contribution.

✓ **Develop a year-round plan** for volunteer recognition, acknowledging that it is an ongoing process.

✓ **Delegate and assign responsibility** for implementing the recognition plan.

✓ **Maintain accurate records** for all volunteers. Include kinds of work done and hours of service, accomplishments and anecdotal comments, as these form the basis for promoting volunteers, writing meaningful letters of reference and, of course, appropriate recognition!

# Informal Recognition Ideas

Many opportunities for creative recognition exist in a volunteer's life cycle. It is important to recognize volunteers throughout the year and at different stages of their involvement.

☐ **At the time they sign up as a volunteer**
- A welcome letter from the President of the organization.
- Assign a buddy or mentor to provide personal support.
- Wrap up a miniature flashlight with a note " Welcome to a bright light".
- A package of tea saying "Since you've joined our group, things are really brewing!"

☐ **On a daily or weekly basis**
- Take time to talk, smile, say "we missed you".

☐ **Each month**
- Highlight a "volunteer of the month", articles in newsletter.
- Chairs might institute a fun "committee member of the month" award.
- Review objectives and celebrate accomplishments.

☐ **On an annual basis**
- Special events, pot luck suppers, Volunteer Week social activities.
- Annual update of service accomplishments and fund-raising results.
- Collage of candid photos of all volunteers displayed at the AGM.

☐ **Upon completion of a special assignment**
- Fill a wine glass with candy and attach a card with the message, "A Toast to a Job Well Done!"
- A box of chocolate kisses, "Take a bow, you deserve a kiss!"
- A glue stick with a note "Thanks for holding us together"

☐ **On special occasions in the volunteer's life**
- Send a card for birthdays, on the anniversary of being a new recruit.

☐ **When they leave**
- Something meaningful to them personally as a reminder and invitation to return.
- Exit interview that affirms their contribution and seeks their wise advice.
- Letter of reference highlighting accomplishments and contribution.

☐ **How do you recognize staff who work well with volunteers?**
- Recognition events should be shared.
- Performance appraisals for staff should take into account their successful work with volunteers.

# Bibliography

K. Blanchard and S. Johnson, *The One Minute Manager*, Avon Books, New York, 1982.

W. Bridges, *Managing Transitions, Making the Most of Change*, Addison-Wesley, Toronto, 1991

S. Ellis, *From the Top Down*, Energize Associates, Philadelphia, 1986.

R. Fisher and W. Ury, *Getting to Yes*, Penguin Books, New York, 1981.

T. Kayser, *Mining Group Gold*, Pfeiffer and Co., Toronto, 1990.

D. Kinlaw, *Coaching for Commitment*, Pfeiffer and Co., Toronto, 1989.

J. Kouzes and B. Posner, *The Leadership Challenge*, Jossey-Bass Publishing, San Francisco, 1987.

R. Lynch, "Designing Volunteer Jobs for Results", *Voluntary Action Leadership*, Summer, 1983.

N. MacDufff, *Episodic Volunteering*, MBA Publishing, Walla Walla, 1991.

M. MacKenzie, *Dealing with Difficult Volunteers*, VMSystems, Heritage Arts Publishing, Downers Grove, 1990.

S. McCurley and R. Lynch, *Essential Volunteer Management*, VMSystems, Downers Grove, 1989.

S. McCurley, *Recruiting for Difficult or Long Term Assignments*, VMSystems, Downers Grove, 1991.

T. Nolan, L. Goodstein, and W. Pfeiffer, *Plan or Die*, Pfeiffer and Co., Toronto, 1993.

I. Scheier, *Staff/Volunteer Relations Collection*, Energize Press, Philadelphia, 1988.

T. Seita, *Leadership Skills for the New Age of Non Profits*, Heritage Arts, Downers Grove, 1990

T. Seita and S. Waechter, *Change: Meet It and Greet It*, Heritage Arts, Downers Grove, 1991.

S. Vineyard, *Evaluating Volunteers, Programs and Events*, Heritage Arts Publishing, Downers Grove, 1988.

S. Vineyard, *Marketing Magic for Volunteer Programs*, Heritage Arts Publishing, Downers Grove, 1984.

M. Wilson, *The Effective Management of Volunteer Programs*, Volunteer Management Associates, Boulder, 1976.

E. Yarbrough, *Constructive Conflict*, VMSystems, Downers Grove, 1988.